Service on the Spectrum

SERVICE

ON THE

SPECTRUM

ASD and Power Exchange

Edited by Joshua Tenpenny

Alfred Press

Hubbardston, Massachusetts

Alfred Press
12 Simond Hill Road
Hubbardston, MA 01452

Service on the Spectrum:
ASD and Power Exchange
© 2022 Joshua Tenpenny
ISBN 979-8-9887309-0-3

Printed in cooperation with
Lulu Enterprises, Inc.
860 Aviation Parkway, Suite 300
Morrisville, NC 27560

Contents

Foreword: The Love/Love Relationship Between My Autism and My Kink

Akasha Eden

This is, first and foremost, a love story. A rom-com, fireworks, boomboxes outside windows at 3 a.m. kind of love story. Symbiosis is such an interesting word, such a fascinating concept. The idea that two species inhabiting space together find such creative ways to survive with, alongside, and even using each other is a wonderful reminder of both the scientific precision and spiritual complexity with which the universe exists. Parasitism and competition are also symbiotic relationships, but as I kept looking, I saw the merits *mutualism* and *communalism* jump out at me from my computer screen.

What, you might ask, do a sappy love story, commensalistic symbiosis, and mutualistic symbiosis have to do with one another?

My autism and my kink. And when I say kink from here on out, it will be an umbrella term for M/s, D/s, fetish, S/m and B&D as I practice and live them. Again, we ask, what do love and symbiosis each have to do with the other?

I firmly believe that I simply wouldn't be here if not for kink, and my autism is an invisible superpower not yet well understood by scientific communities.

14-year-old me is probably looking at this, shaking her head, and wondering when her older self must have gone totally off of the deep end. Autism? A superpower? Looking back, it's pretty easy for me to realize and remember the things that separated me from other children and which made it clear that I was neurodivergent. The toe walking, the tongue chewing, the finger picking, the repetition of sentences until they were perfect if I detected any grammatical or punctuation issues, let alone mispronunciations. The deep, grave sense of impending doom if plans change on a dime, and the feeling of stuckness and stagnation and isolation in the presence of others. I convinced myself that my peers didn't wanna hang out with me because I was better than them, but I had no choice but to maintain that belief system, otherwise I would've collapsed into an even larger pile of self-hating goo. Books were my best friends. Some years, books were my only friend. After being physically assaulted, emotionally or verbally berated, or otherwise bullied by peers or family, the anger would subsume itself into self-hatred and I would immediately go seek out a book. Whatever life was being lived in that book, at least it wasn't mine.

Their Eyes Were Watching God by Zora Neale Hurston is one of the books that I would seek out after a particularly bad incident. Watching the protagonist re-create herself through all kinds of adversity, and with this open, humorous and yet appropriately resigned spirit helped me to begin adopting a similar one, a similar, rooted resilience. The diversity of mental health problems that were displayed in that novel also made me feel seen. It's not as if anyone was talking about the neurodivergence or neurodiversity spectrum, but knowing how long "the town fool" (or that one cousin who is missing a few marbles) had been around, despite their being outdated and offensive tropes now, still made me feel like I was being seen.

My first suicide attempt was at 14 years old. I was tired, to the bone, soul-deep of trying to fit in with people that I didn't understand and who didn't understand me from a deep, fundamental perspective. I was also tired of traversing the PTSD flashbacks and autistic meltdowns all by myself. A migraine? My family was all over it. A dislocated shoulder? They were buzzing around, worried. My mental health troubles? According to them, my high levels of performance in school made it unnecessary to poke around up there or ask any questions. The suicide attempt and the ensuing mandatory year of therapy brought a lot of very uncomfortable questions and answers to the surface. Funnily enough, I would not be diagnosed with autism until my early 20s. Before that it was depression and anxiety. I wouldn't even be diagnosed with PTSD until, again, my early 20s.

Now, at 28 years old, I can safely say that autism is a neurological and neurophysiological condition generally present at birth. A lot of the shame and pain that I felt being different was stripped away once I shone the light of knowledge and destigmatization on those dark parts of myself. Self-compassion. Grace for little Akasha.

Now when I watch my own child walk on her toes and chew her tongue, I don't punish her or discipline her for it. I let her self-stimulate, because I know exactly what she's going through that's making her walk on her toes and making her chew her tongue. After all, I went through the same thing.

When she begins to have trouble with socialization, I will do my best to intercede and let her know that masking is an imperfect solution, but that it's an option if she'd like to socialize with a lot of neurotypical people. A lot of the solutions I will have for her will be imperfect, but I am also confident that at least I have the solutions in mind, the grace to give them to her, and the drive to figure out what I don't yet know. She won't be my guinea pig, like I was for my parents, working through having an autistic child for the first time and treating it like a dirty, shameful and painful family secret.

One thing that still makes me supremely jealous is how easily socialization seems to come to neurotypical people who aren't in some other way undersocialized. To this day I don't know how to make proper eye contact; people either tell me that I am not looking at them often enough, or that I'm looking at them so directly that it makes them uncomfortable. Then of course I have to do that little shuffle in my brain, trying to find the social script that matches best with the tableau in front of me. Wouldn't it be amazing if I just didn't have to? The unwritten social rules of vanilla and Neurotypical society will always confuse me, always.

So this hasn't felt much like a love story thus far, has it? Do you remember that trope, enemies to lovers, where the protagonist meets someone who is supremely annoying or frustrating or hurtful or antagonizing in some other way, and then slowly but surely all those little points of annoyance or frustration begin to fade away as the protagonist realizes that their "enemy" is actually perfect for them?

Cue my autism. I began to realize that often, in a group of people around the same age, I would be the most intelligent and most experienced, I had to begin interrogating why I felt that way and whether that was backed up by fact. I became a licensed attorney at 24 years old, I have a doctorate degree and master's degree, and the hyper focus and creative approaches to problem-solving that come with my neurodivergence are, in large part, the traits that enabled me to accomplish those goals as quickly as I did.

It took a lot of both external and internal examination of self in order to get to a place where I can acknowledge that the facts of my life are not normal, not just because I'm autistic, but because I am impressive. If you look inside my brain right now, my self-hatred would still be popping up and saying boo, but when I can use facts like those to quiet it down, you can see how it's effective. For my neurodivergent and low-self-esteem friends, read this out loud with me:

I find myself beautiful, and worthy. I have value. I love myself, and that's all that matters. Self-love is the most important love of them all. I am my own soulmate. I am not defined by the actions or behavior of other people. I matter. I am worthy of being communicated with, and being kept informed. I am worthy of that respect and courtesy. But whether or not I get that respect and courtesy, I will give myself that respect and courtesy, and I will value the love I can give to myself, because knowing myself, it is a beautiful and worthy love.

I will not act rashly, nor will I speak rashly, nor will I repeat myself. I will not. My voice is precious to me, because I love myself. My time is precious to me, because I love myself. Even if others might not value me, I will value myself. Even if others don't follow given and decided upon plans, I will follow my plan. I am in control of my destiny. I am in control of my person, and my whereabouts. My plan is what becomes my life. I love my life, because I love myself. I treasure myself, and I genuinely like my personality, body, and face more than I like that of others. I love myself above all others. Only I matter when it comes to self-care and self-prioritization. And I put all of my considerable store of resources into that valuing process, because the world is a terrible, terrible place where people can be stupid, cruel, ignorant monsters.

I treasure my friends, because they are there when I need them, and when I call them or make plans with them, they follow through with those plans. They communicate with me if they'll be late or unavailable to talk, which is why we're friends. We have lots of great memories together that I value deeply, and they've each taught me different things, and I love each of them in their own way.

If you read it out loud, thank you. I'm sure a big part of yourself thanks you too, one that you don't get to see or hear from very often.

But here's a question that I get a lot when teaching, and one that forms a big part of many of my presentations, because I think it's important to differentiate the feelings of isolation and sadness that a lot of Univision people experience in the mainstream social scene versus what it is that we do.

What do I mean by the social contract?

A social contract, according to the Oxford English-language dictionary, is an implicit agreement among the members of a society to cooperate for social benefits—for example, by sacrificing some individual freedom for state protection. Theories of a social contract became popular in the 16th, 17th, and 18th centuries among philosophers such as Thomas Hobbes, John Locke, and Jean-Jacques Rousseau, as a means of explaining the origin of government and the obligations of subjects.

That is the moral, political, and philosophical definition, but boiled down to its essentials, social contract theory explains that people give up individual freedom in exchange for peace and protection, and otherwise people would live in a state of anarchy under natural law, meeting every man, woman or person for themselves.

But what does that mean when it comes to the vanilla or mainstream social contract? Simply put, in order to have friends, family, and other social connections, approve of, and take care of us in an interdependent society, we need to conform. We need to act in a way that pleases, and does not frighten or threaten society or our social circles. This is the mainstream social contract. When people enter kink, they are in a lot of ways explicitly rejecting the mainstream social contract, and the exchange of freedom of self-determination and freedom from social pressure to conform in order to fully be themselves. When we look at certain autistic behaviors (like masking) it becomes that much more clear why the kink community is in some ways a safer haven for neurodiverse people, as so many of us gangsters have to mask for many years, until we can strip them off and completely be ourselves in kink spaces for the first time.

The thing that really appealed to me when I first discovered the kink community was the respect for bodily autonomy which is built into the framework. When you first come into the community, there are tons of workshops and mentors and information handouts even on how to negotiate the BDSM scene. You're not supposed to touch anybody without their enthusiastic and explicit consent, and when you do engage in an activity with someone, it is first discussed with an exploration of what is and isn't okay to do, and how it is going to be done. As an autistic person, this new social contract was like nirvana. I felt building blocks of confidence taking hold, piece by piece. I felt able to tackle the world while backed by this new social contract.

Now let's turn our eyes to some of the meat and potatoes of how and why kink welcomed and then enveloped me in its joyful, loving and open arms, creating that commensalistic symbiotic relationship where my autism helps me survive, and I help my autism to survive. To be completely open, comorbid with my autism, I suffer from sensory processing disorder. At its worst, you might see me wearing earmuffs or AirPods or full-on gun range ear protectors in order to protect myself from unwanted auditory stimuli. At its best, you'll see me being flipped upside down in a single ankle gravity boot by one of my favorite rope Tops during my class on spiritual rope, and orgasm three times while upside down from the sensation of the rope and the spinning and the connection between the two of us. Sensory play is a huge part of BDSM.

Many people will use padded restraints so that they can feel tightly bound, unable to move-yet without experiencing any pain. (Sensory deprivation! My favorite thing.) Some will use hoods and earplugs, blindfolds, mummification bags and even padded mittens, to limit the sensory input the person is experiencing so they can focus on one specific sensation being given to them by their Top. This could be as simple as the sensation of sharp nails raking gently over your back, the use of a violet wand (which creates a static-type sensation), or soft rabbit fur and other textures rubbed on the skin, all of which are much easier to process when it is the only sensation the bottom has to deal with. For those of us in the room who have sensory processing disorders, consider the joy and catharsis that many of us experienced for the first time being in a predicament, bondage, or sensory deprivation situation with a top that was completely negotiated, had clear signposts, clear safe words, clear boundaries, clear guards on what to do in almost every possible given (negative or positive) situation, and then consider how that same scene might have gone under the vanilla social contract, and in the main stream, sexual or sensual context. Too many times, I see choking happening during a spanking between vanilla people who have not pre-negotiated or pre-consented to any of these activities. While these may be activities that we, especially as a pertains to choking in the community, consider deep edgeplay, we sit down and consider the risks and do our best to mitigate and manage them.

Even though at this point we still might want to conclude that this is actually a love-hate relationship, I have made my peace with the mainstream social contract and left it behind. I realize it is deeply imperfect, just like us, which means that it doesn't have power over me, and even further than that has no way of reaching me when I am in the loving arms of kink. I'm in a place now where I don't hate the things about myself that mean that I am autistic. I honor them and mean them nothing but good, almost the exact same way I feel about my ancestors. My autism is a part of me that I would never give up, that I love for what it is, and that has led me to experiences beyond my wildest dreams. See? Love. Symbiosis.

That my friends, is why my relationship with autism is a love/love relationship, and nothing more, and nothing less.

Autism can be a beautiful thing. Many of the traits associated with autism are actually huge strengths that can help individuals thrive and make amazing contributions to our world. Take creativity, for example. People on the autism spectrum often have tremendous creative talent! They may express this in multiple ways, from painting masterpieces to solving complex technical problems. With their out-of-the-box thinking, they can come up with solutions that no one else has thought of before.

People on the autism spectrum also tend to approach situations logically and rationally, which can be beneficial in many areas from organization and problem solving to understanding complex topics quickly. This logical thinking allows them to look at things without any bias or preconceived notions, which can be incredibly useful in certain conditions.

Individuals on the autism spectrum are often known for their focus and attention to detail. They may be able to pay attention to small details that others would miss, and this can be a great asset in many fields such as research, law, medicine or engineering. Additionally, they may also have high levels of concentration (the good old hyperfocus) that allows them to stay focused on tasks for longer than others might.

These are just some of the strengths associated with autism—there are so many more! People on the autism spectrum have so much to offer, and can do amazing things when given the right opportunities and proper, culturally competent support. It's time we start recognizing these traits as the invisible superpowers that they are, and really celebrating the power and value of our diversity!

Introduction

Greetings, readers.

My name is Joshua Tenpenny, and I am a non-binary, transmasculine, male-presenting person with a variety of autistic spectrum issues; and I've been in an intentional power dynamic relationship for nineteen years.

My master Raven and I generally think of ourselves as "Owner" and "property", defining it as a relationship where he has complete authority over everything in my life. We often use the words "Master" and "slave" when we talk to people outside our household, because those are the terms most commonly used. Raven also calls me his "boy", though he's not my "daddy", and it is arguable whether that is an appropriate term for me from a Leather perspective. But Raven has been calling his male/butch/transmasculine/etc. submissives "boy" since 1993, and he's unlikely to change that any time soon.

Raven has authority over my body, my diet, my medical decisions, my job, my education, my vote, and my religion—and everything else in between. That didn't all come at once—I slowly gave over areas of my life as I (or he, in some cases) felt comfortable with it. We kept communicating about it all the way through, and we see ourselves as part of a team, colluding together to make this power dynamic work for both of us.

I was eventually given an official diagnosis of Autistic Spectrum Disorder in my mid-20s, but it has been clear there was something "off" about me since I was a small child. My relatives often commented on how strange and disconnected I seemed, off in my own world. I was routinely chastised for playing with my toys "wrong"—mostly arranging, sorting, and stacking them, with no imaginative play. I preferred sorting Lite-Brite pegs by color to actually using them to make pictures, and I had no idea what to do with dolls or action figures. When I was anxious, I liked to tear whole paper catalogs into tiny bits, which my mother said was "like living with a hamster". My fondness for the color generally referred to as "school-bus-yellow" came from a toy unicorn I was given which had yellow velveteen feet; I would lie around and rub its soft yellow feet on my face, which I now know to be "stimming", using sensation to calm one's nervous system.

I struggled a lot with my emotions as a teenager, and sex was one of the very few things that really helped me feel better. It was also my primary motivation for developing social skills. I was largely indifferent to spending time with other people for much of my childhood, but in my early teens I realized that if I was going to actually have sex with anyone, I would probably have to, you know... talk to them.

I got involved in the Rocky Horror Picture Show, which provided a venue for a wide variety of weirdo teenagers to explore sexuality in a largely unsupervised environment. It was where I met my first (ex) master, lost my virginity, and experimented with gender presentation. There were fewer genuinely kinky folks there than I had hoped, but it was my entry into the kink scene.

It wasn't until fairly recently that I realized a big part of my struggles with romantic relationships has been that I am essentially aromantic. I very much enjoy sex, but I've never really cared much whether I had an emotional connection to my sexual partners. I'm not strongly invested in forming platonic friendships either. I can enjoy the company of others, but all things being equal, I prefer to spend most of my time alone. While I did eventually fall in love with Raven, in my previous long-term relationships, I was affectionate but not at all emotionally invested. From my perspective, I didn't see any difference between a long-term "romantic" partner, and a roommate I was having sex with. I was vaguely aware there was supposed to be a difference, but didn't really understand it. Even with Raven, our relationship is first and foremost a working service relationship centered around the power dynamic, with the emotional part a very fulfilling component, but not an essential one.

In general, I am most comfortable in situations where it is unambiguous who is in charge, and clearly know the scope of their authority. I was really surprised when my master's daughter referred to me as "bossy", but in a situation where there is no clear authority figure, I often find myself taking charge, even though I prefer to follow someone else's lead. I just find it extremely difficult (and stressful) to come to a consensus or compromise among "equals". From my perspective, people are never really just "equals". They always have multiple different levels and types of influence over each other, different types of power that they may or may not choose to bring to bear, and the whole thing is a very complex and largely unspoken dance that I have never felt comfortable with. I just want to lay all my cards on the table, and have an established protocol for reaching a fair decision. In my one long-term relationship (eight years) with an "equal" partner, it was constant power struggles, and I felt like I had to be constantly on guard to make sure I got my "fair share". Being able to let go of that was one of the biggest benefits to me of my relationship with Raven.

When I first started looking at power exchange, it was the structured aspect that appealed to me. As a teenager, I'd flirted with the idea of joining the military (despite being an asthmatic nerd girl) or a monastery (despite not being remotely religious). Like many neurodiverse folks, my craving for structure greatly surpasses my ability to actually sustain a structured routine, so having some kind of external structure seemed ideal.

Unfortunately, my master Raven is one of the least structured people around. He'll grudgingly tolerate structure when it makes things markedly easier, but in general he finds it stifling, boring, and annoying. The early parts of our relationship were fraught with me wishing he was more like the very detail-oriented masters I read about. (Bob Rubel was my image of the perfect master.) I desperately wanted someone who was very particular about the forks being lined up precisely when the table was set, and I wound up with someone who found it rarely necessary to set a table at all.

However, it isn't that he didn't train me in anything. He noticed quickly how uneven my social skills were, and also couldn't help noticing my sensory issues and other weird habits. Unlike my previous partners who didn't know what to make of me, Raven had friends on the spectrum, and eventually broached the subject to me. It was useful, and somewhat comforting, to know that when I had autistic-spectrum problems, it was just my neurology and not some terrible character flaw. I complained about the fact that my master didn't want to "train" me like the demanding regimens of fictional slaves in gay leather novels, but eventually I realized that he was subtly training me the whole time. It wasn't in how to set formal tables or walk six paces behind; it was how to be kind and considerate to him and appropriate with outsiders. Well, and also how he likes everything in his life done for him, even though it's usually the "wrong way" in my mind. Don't let my tone here fool you, though—there is no one I have ever met whom I would prefer to be in service to. We are an amazingly good fit on so many levels. He sees me for who I am, understands me, works with me, encourages me to improve myself, and gives me purpose in life.

Speaking of some of that purpose: My master had been teaching in the kink community since long before I entered his service, and he was very clever about getting me involved. Raven started by inviting me to sit in the front row during his classes, and encouraged me to participate. Then he had me sit next to him, but assured me I didn't have to say anything at all. He'd drop lines that he knew I had something to say about, and leave space for me to jump in, but didn't ask me direct questions. Next, for a class where I had routinely made comments, he'd directly ask me to speak on a point. He provided the framework and made use of my perspective within it, and taught me how to pass the "microphone" smoothly back and forth between us. Eventually, he had me teaching along with him, and after a few years, on my own. I have a good deal of social anxiety, but I found that presenting on a topic I am confident of, in front of a receptive audience of strangers is actually much easier for me than a casual social encounter with the exact same people.

Teaching about M/s in the greater demographic meant that we traveled a lot and met a variety of new people on a regular basis. We joined our local MAsT group, and eventually won the 2014 Northeast Master/slave competition, which was essentially a year-long grant with a mandate to teach anywhere we could; in that year we logged over 14,000 miles. We also began to offer peer counseling for new M/s couples who were having difficulty, and during all this community involvement we began to notice something. People on the spectrum showed up time and time again in these relationships, on both sides of the slash.

The further we go down this road and the greater our involvement with power dynamic folks online and off, the more we notice how ASD is overrepresented in the M/s demographic. Over and over, we run into autistic M-types who are using the relationship structure to manage coping with the outside world, and autistic s-types who are using it for structure, and both of them sing the praises of a relationship style which mandates that it be custom-built, intensively negotiated, and often full of rules. Again and again, we hear, "In this relationship, I don't have to guess!"

That's why we decided to put together this book. In our previous books *Broken Toys* and *Mastering Mind*, we had sections where we discussed masters and slaves on the spectrum, but we now believe that it's common enough that it needs its own book, with the words of a variety of different people in it. This is our gift to you. You're not alone, and you can do this.

Joshua Tenpenny
Hubbardston, MA 2023

Slaves on the Spectrum

Care and Managing of the ASD Submissive

Raven Kaldera and Joshua Tenpenny

(*This article is reprinted—and slightly edited—from the anthology* Broken Toys: Submissives with Mental Illness or Neurological Dysfunction, *and originated on the "Broken Toys" website over a decade ago.*)

Raven: I've had my slaveboy Joshua for nigh on a dozen years now. He's smart, detail-oriented, hard-working, and eager to please. He's alphabetized my pantry, designed my websites, and done a million other wonderful tasks that make my life easier. He's also on the high end of the autism spectrum; when we first wrote this essay, I wrote that he had Asperger's Syndrome. (The DSM-IV has now decided to roll Asperger's into the full Autistic Spectrum Disorder, regardless of functioning, largely because of the grey area between "Aspie" and "not-Aspie", and the difficulty in diagnosing borderline cases, but many Aspies still refer to themselves that way, while others prefer not to do so. Your mileage may vary.) This means that he sometimes needs special handling. In order to manage him in the most effective way, I have to take his disability into account.

Unlike a simple physical condition (like a bad back or arthritic hands), this is a subtle and pervasive condition, popping up in all sorts of interesting places in his reactions, preferences, and mental obstacles. When he does something irritating or strange, one of the first questions I have to ask is, "Is this an ASD thing I just haven't nailed down yet?" There's a fair chance that it is, and a master cannot blame their s-type for their inborn neurological wiring. Not only is that unfair, but it removes any hope of finding an effective compensatory behavior.

Autistic spectrum disorders vary widely in both range of symptoms and severity, and while the two of us hope that this article will prove useful to dominant types with s-types on the spectrum, we also realize that we cannot hope to cover every problem or issue, nor will the ones that we discuss necessarily be relevant to every couple. Some folks on the spectrum posit the existence of at least two different "flavors" of disorder, for example—one that is more logical and

"Spocklike", with difficulty being aware of and expressing emotion; and one that is highly emotionally expressive and reactive. (For more information on this, read *The Unwritten Rules of Social Relationships: Decoding Social Mysteries Through the Unique Perspective of Autism* by Temple Grandin and Sean Barron, who are examples of these two different forms.) At any rate, your autistic s-type may well go through this article and find some problems that they do have, and others that they don't. They may also have problems we didn't go into, although we've not yet met one who didn't have issues with their sensory "filter" getting overloaded a lot sooner than that of a neurotypical individual. As with any disability in a slave or submissive, it's the M-type's job to find out anything they can about that disability … and it's the s-type's job to aid them in that discovery, through both research and personal transparency.

Not every dominant is going to want to take on a submissive or slave with ASD. If you're the kind of person for whom the ability to figure out what you want and have it given to you without your asking is a signature of love or commitment to the relationship, you will probably be continually disappointed. If you are stuck on having someone whose emotional reactions are simultaneously socially normal and genuine, you may also want to think again. If you're not interested in "motoring them through" (a term for physically training autistic children often used by their parents) situations that most people would react normally to, then you might want to look elsewhere. However, if none of these obstacles (and the others I'll go into in this article) bother you in the least, then by all means go ahead. For myself, I'm happy to train my slave how to act in any situation, so long as I know he'll do what I say to the best of his ability, which he does.

Joshua: ASD people can have a wide range of life skills, but their social/emotional development is generally rather uneven. I know that when my master got me, he was shocked by the contrast between situations I could handle gracefully and those where I was entirely clueless.

By the time they reach adulthood, many ASD folks may be very good at faking it, but in a close relationship you'll likely be able to see the holes in their understanding. For example, I had very little conception of what love, trust, or intimacy actually felt like when my master first got me. Without the power dynamic, I would not have been able to develop that understanding, because I didn't desire emotional intimacy and I didn't see what the allure of it was all about. In my previous relationships, it was either not expected of me (as in my first master) or my partner was constantly frustrated with his acts of intimacy not being reciprocated (as in my long-term egalitarian partner; I liked him fine, but didn't understand what emotional connection he expected). I wasn't connected to my family, either; I liked them, and I knew they cared about me, but for instance I never understood why the other kids at summer camp missed their families.

However, my current master was able to get into my head and pull me into those emotions. There was an early stage when I didn't quite understand what he was subtly motoring me through, but in an egalitarian partnership I would have broken it off, where here I simply followed orders and walked right into the intimacy maze because my master told me to do so, and I was invested in being obedient. I was also very self-enclosed due to a fear of vulnerability, but in an M/s relationship I was rewarded for being vulnerable, so it opened me up in ways I didn't know could happen.

This was helped by our mutual discipline of radical honesty with each other, which only could have been done successfully in an M/s setting. If I didn't have a partner who could—and would—specifically tell me how to phrase things in a more kind manner, and whose word I would absolutely follow, radical honesty would have become a venue for verbal abuse, as I have a hard time understanding which words do and don't hurt people.

Overstimulation

Raven: One of the problems that ASD shares to an extent with ADD is having a too-permeable filter. On an ordinary day, most neurotypical people automatically shut out up to 80% of their stimuli—appliance noises, electric hums, moving shadows, bright colors, the shifting of clothing on the body—but one of the prime symptoms of ASD is a filter that won't shut out enough to function for long periods in a high-stimulus environment. When the edge of overstimulation is reached, people on the autistic spectrum often have stronger emotional responses to it than most adults with ADD, for example—including, sometimes, freaking out. Their version of freaking out may be atypical; if you've got one of the less emotionally expressive sorts, you might not even know that they've been freaking out for several minutes until they blow up over some small thing. The more emotionally expressive sorts may freak out with unusual gestures and noises. Most have learned to leave and find a quiet place when the edge is looming, but if they are "on duty" and not free to run off when necessary, the M-type has to make that decision for them.

As an example of how we handle this, Joshua has a special hand signal that he uses when he is on duty in public and has reached his limit of stimulation. Even if he's serving in the middle of a loud party, I know that if he gives me that signal, it's time to let him go sit in a quiet place for a while, or he will soon be worse than useless. (I also trust him implicitly to never use that signal unless he is actually nearing the end of his rope; he wants very much to do a good job at whatever I ask.) The hand signal is not something that others might interpret, so I can say, "Josh, go do X," and he can go calm his mind without having to mention his issues in front of people. (He's uncomfortable with discussing his ASD problems in public in party situations, less out of humiliation and more because of the unhelpful ways that well-meaning people try to accommodate or assist him, or because he's found that people often interpret it as a negative judgment on the situation, reading it as: "Your party is too loud and you are talking about things that upset me so much that I have to leave.")

Loud, confusing crowd noise is only one of the host of sensory issues that may dog an autistic individual. I've had it described to me by my slaveboy and other Aspie friends as living every day under a barrage of sensations that they must constantly struggle to block out and focus around, and while many of them have learned to do that, it eats up a lot of their resources. Certain textures can be like torture—itchy clothing tags, slimy food; each person on the spectrum may have their own list of texture-hates. That can, in some cases or on particularly bad days, become other people's skin or even their own;

my slaveboy's central nervous system is aggravated by allergic reactions (which makes the ASD symptoms worse) and there have been days when he can't stand to touch himself, much less me. On those days, sexual service is pretty much out; we've managed at best to snuggle with a smooth, soft sheet between us.

Some folks on the spectrum can't look at certain visual patterns without mental discomfort; others become hypnotized by visual patterns. (I've lost Joshua in the grocery store, only to find him staring glazedly at a geometric arrangement of cereal boxes.) Some find certain sounds unblockable, as nerve-wracking as fingernails on a blackboard. In fact, one common symptom of this disorder is that their "startle reflex" doesn't turn off when it should. You know the physical response your body has when someone sets off a firecracker or slams something loudly behind you? Imagine that it went off a few dozen times a day, five times more intensely, and then kept going for several minutes no matter how you tried to calm yourself. I've got Aspie friends who can't ever be around recreational target gunfire for this reason.

As an example of sonic sensory issues, my slaveboy can't stand the sound of plastic bags crackling. If he is driving me on a shopping trip and the wind is blowing our plastic shopping bags in the back seat, and he asks to be allowed to stop and tamp them down … well, I can refuse him and make him keep driving and deal with it, but I'll have to understand the consequences. Does he have the resources to keep driving with that crackling noise going on? Yes. Does he have the resources to cope with crackling plastic, driving, and being anything but grouchy, distressed, and largely nonverbal? No. Will he have the resources to recover from that distressing drive immediately upon coming home? Probably not. This is why I say that I do not compromise with my slave, but sometimes I have to compromise with reality. I've learned what his nervous system can tolerate and what it can't. He's willing to push himself to that limit for me; he depends on my honor and common sense not to push him beyond it.

In terms of S/M: Some folks on the spectrum have told me how a good beating smooths out their central nervous system, overriding the built-up tensions, and calms them down. Others—like my slaveboy—have anomalous random responses to physical stimuli. Any stimulus, from itching to orgasms to pain—what feels good on one day can feel terrible and almost traumatizing on another, and there's no way to know until you do it, so S/M is something of a minefield. Make sure you find out which type you've got before you start playing with them.

Joshua: For me, overstimulation is about knowing what is a drain on my mental resources. My resources are not infinite, and if I can remove some excess stimulation, I have more resources left to do my job. Previous to me really understanding this diagnosis, I would tune out many of the things I found annoying because other people didn't seem to be bothered by them. After coming to terms with my diagnosis, I became much more willing to look at that. Now I'll assess whether I can cut myself some slack with regard to avoiding stimuli, or in being OK with a less perfect final product when I am working in a difficult situation.

With our M/s relationship, we had to find a balance between my master setting up special circumstances for me to work at my best, and him inconveniencing himself in order to do so. We found through trial and error that there was only so far he was willing to go with that, and so he decides how much he's willing to let imperfect circumstances affect my productivity. I've also found that if am able to reduce most of the sources of stimulation over a long period of time, it helps me to focus better, but it also makes me more sensitive to it in the long run. Smaller things become almost as annoying as the larger things, and then if I have to deal with a chaotic outside environment, it becomes really awful. So being in a somewhat chaotic home environment instead of a perfect greenhouse actually keeps my tolerance up.

It also helped me understand that the overstimulation is my problem. It's not that the people who are at this party are so terrible, it's that I am having trouble coping with it. Before my diagnosis, I would blame the external people and circumstances for my distress, and I couldn't see how different my responses were from those of other people. The M/s relationship with Raven was the first time I'd had someone pay that much attention to my inner process—especially someone who had the authority to order my behavior.

After reading about Dr. Temple Grandin's squeeze machine—a mechanism based on something used to calm down cows, which she built in order to get her nervous system calmed down—I made myself a rock blanket. It's a sturdy canvas quilt of pockets, and each one holds a plastic bag of gravel. I lay it on myself when I need nervous-system calming; even all-over pressure is a classic tool that ASD people use to calm themselves down. Sometimes I have had Raven lay on top of me, which was wonderful, but he's the master and he gets bored and wanders off. Still, the rock blanket is there when I need it, because I never have to worry that it is bored.

Then there's the issue of eye contact. Many ASD people have trouble with any kind of sustained eye contact—one memorably described it as: "We're having the meeting on Wednesday—Eyeballs! Eyeballs! Eyeballs!—um, uh, I think I can make it—Eyeballs! Eyeballs! Eyeballs!" and so on. The human gaze is just so neurologically overstimulating that it turns the brain off and we can't talk. I've learned ways to do it obliquely in social situations, but the kind of sustained eye contact that masters often want is just hard for us. I remember being at a M/s weekend intensive, with another slave on the spectrum and her master right beside us. The teachers had us all do an exercise where we held eye contact and communicated our feelings. It made the other couples all lovey-gooshy. It made me and the other slave very, very uncomfortable and kind of freaked out. Both our masters are sadists, though, and they knew how far they could push us before letting us go, as we quivered like bugs under a needle and had to shake and breathe for a while. For me, intense eye contact with my master is as mentally overwhelming as being grabbed by the throat. It can be hot, in a way, but I can't have a coherent conversation. (I don't suggest playing sadistically with your s-type's ASD triggers until you've been together a long time and you are both fine with it, though.)

Literality and Precision of Instructions

Raven: While—again—every individual on the spectrum is different, one frequent frustration that new autistic s-types have with masters is that the orders they give are too vague. Many masters, upon hearing this, may raise their eyebrows—"My orders aren't vague!"—

but they underestimate how literally and specifically these folks take those orders. The classic "example joke" about the new sub on the spectrum is that the M-type tells them to fetch a glass of water, and they wander back empty-handed saying, "There are no clean glasses—will a mug do?" They probably stood there and agonized over whether the M-type intended them to take the time to clean a glass, thus fulfilling the order literally but taking up a lot of time, or put the water in a coffee mug which was "wrong". Some might default to the first choice, leaving the master wondering where they vanished to and how long it could take to simply get them some water, or default to the second with apprehensive tears in their eyes, genuinely fearing to be reprimanded because it wasn't an actual glass.

While this may seem oversimplified, literalities like this may trip them up all the time, and it isn't the least bit amusing to them. It's stressful, and they often have lower stress thresholds than neurotypical folks, because their entire environment is so often a source of constant low-level stress that the buffer gets used up quickly. On the other hand, if you've got the precise and meticulous sort of s-type on the spectrum who loves specific instructions, you can have anything exactly the way that you want it, if you just put in the time to make things detail-oriented. One master of an ASD slave told me that her slave never made her morning coffee the way she liked it. Upon questioning him, it turned out that he wasn't sure exactly how she liked it, because while he'd seen her make coffee for herself, she seemed to do things a little differently each time and she hadn't ever described her exact method. Given this confusion, he reverted to making her coffee the way he had previously learned as the "correct" way. I suggested that if she were to take the time to figure out and write up the exact procedure for making her coffee, and hang it up right next to the coffee maker, both parties would get exactly what they wanted—correct coffee for her, and the comfort of a "correct method" for him.

This, of course, means that masters have to learn to give more precise instructions, and masters of both genders often become disgruntled when told that they have to change how they issue orders and instructions. Many of them—especially the more emotionally-oriented types with a strong sense of subtlety—will be very uncomfortable with what may feel to them as being forced into a precise "mechanical" style. However, this is the same issue that the dominant of any disabled s-type runs into: sometimes one has to compromise with the disability, or nothing will get done. (It's important, though, to discern over time what is an unchangeable side effect of the disability and what can be slowly worked on with time.) One possible aid might be getting a third party who is good at breaking down instructions into a more precise form, and having them "translate" the master's rules, perhaps into a written rulebook. At any rate, even if the master isn't normally the sort to write things down, most ASD s-types do better with a written rulebook that they can refer to, and be sure they are doing things right. Knowing that if they just do X they'll always be correct is very comforting to them.

Joshua: It is important not to let the "clarification of instructions" become a power struggle. You should be aware of whether they are really just trying to find out what you want, or whether they are using a search for "clarification" as a way to obstructively react to an order they disagree with. Observe them over time to figure out the difference, and don't let it become manipulative. If you as the master are feeling pressured to give them more specific instructions, watch to see if simple clarification helps their genuine confusion, or if it's starting to feel like a negotiation about how you will give them orders—in which case, shut it down.

Also, if you want to teach them how to generalize this from other situations, you can prompt them—"What do you think I would want in this situation? Based on what you've seen of me, what do you think I prefer?" If they get it right, great; if they get it wrong, just correct them and move on. If they seem to be tripping up on the basic concept that you are not them and don't want what they want, that's a bigger issue that needs to be addressed separately. If they seem clear on that basic concept, make it clear that you want them to observe how you do things and take note of your preferences. (They may need to actually write these things down.) Prompt them to extrapolate in new situations. Take time to train them to respond how you want. You want, ideally, for them to come to a place of using good critical thinking skills and showing insight into your preferences, and at the same time not using their confusion as a way to get out of things. If they have emotional baggage from a lifetime of people whose reactions were opaque (and who were not willing to work with them) and they've given up on understanding anyone but themselves, you may find resistance to this progression.

My suggestion to masters in this situation is that they ask the s-type to propose a few different methods, and then the master picks one. If you routinely just have them propose one method, because you don't really care exactly how it is done, that can be detrimental in the long term to their sense of submission. By having them suggest multiple possibilities, you make it less likely that they would feel like they were just doing what they wanted anyway, and more likely that both of you will get something you want out of the situation.

Rigidity

Raven: For many s-types on the spectrum, as long as they have specific rules to go by—rules about how to act, how to speak, how the relationship is to be run—they really don't care whether the rules match anything considered socially "normal", or even currently in existence outside the household. This can make them remarkably easy-going when it comes to unusual relationship styles such as polyamory or long-distance relationships, so long as they can be entirely sure what they can expect, and how they should respond. Sometimes, however, they get hung up on another chronic ASD problem: rigidity.

Because they have trouble figuring out heavily social-mandate-laden or social-emotion-laden patterns, they tend to figure out one specific way to do a specific activity that someone (perhaps their parents) have told them is Right, and they cling to that method for dear life. Changing structures can also be excruciatingly difficult for them, making it even more of a challenge to get them to learn a new way of frying bacon, or hanging laundry, or assembling your sandwich. If the instructions are specific enough and your s-type is still resistant, suspect this issue.

However, part of being an s-type is that one has to adapt at least to some extent to the master's patterns. It is quite possible for someone on the spectrum to adapt to a new way of doing things; practice and building a new "rut" works just like it does for anyone else. They may need extra support, though, and appreciation of the fact that it's extra difficult for them, and lots of patience.

Joshua: It would not be unusual for an otherwise submissive and obedient ASD s-type to argue at length over the correct way to hang pants, perhaps even citing various expert sources to support their method or repeatedly detailing the flaws in the master's preferred method. The master may naturally think, "Why do they care? Why can't they just hang my damn pants the way I want them hung?"

One useful method for handling this might be to say, "First prove to me you can do it my way—that you are willing and able to obey me in this—and after three months, I will consider the method you suggested. Your obedience is more important to me than creased pants. Until then, no comments or suggestions about how to handle laundry." Understanding relative priorities is hard for many ASD folks, and they may need it spelled out. The time period is important, so they can attempt to put it out of their mind until then. Having a very clear definition of what, exactly, you've declared off-limits is also important. A general statement like "I don't want to hear about this again!" is likely to be interpreted too narrowly by the ASD s-type, leading them to think that only one specific aspect of the issue is off-limits.

If there are specific types of responses you find annoying, the ASD s-type may not able to effectively generalize the concept of, for instance, "Don't be such a pedantic ass about trivial shit!" You can attempt to describe exactly what you mean, but it may be more effective to pick a consistent phrase you use for that particular type of annoying behavior (such as "pedantic ass") and each time they do it, clearly point it out using the same phrasing. Interrupt them while they are doing it, and say, "That! That right there is what I mean by being a pedantic ass." Even if they are not consistently able to prevent the behavior, they should be able to learn to identify when they are doing it. There is rarely any good reason to allow them to argue about why you oughtn't find a certain behavior annoying, whether this ought to count as an instance of that annoying behavior, or what term you ought to use to describe the behavior. Just be consistent, and point it out every time you notice it.

Alternatively, some ASD s-types do very well with a "Because I'm the boss and I said so" approach. It may be easier to convince an s-type on the spectrum that their master, for some unknown reason, prefers their pants hung the "wrong" way, than it is to convince them that the master's way is "right". The master may not like the s-type seeing their way as "wrong", but to put it in perspective, consider that ASD people routinely fail to understand the complexity of other people's motivations. The s-type may already believe that their master, like nearly everyone else in the world, continually does things "wrong" (illogically, inefficiently, etc.) for no discernible reason, and that society in general is full of bizarre and conflicting layers of inscrutable, ridiculous rules.

An older, more experienced, or more introspective s-type may genuinely want to understand why their master wants things a certain way, but it is likely to be quite a struggle for them to understand and accept their master's priorities and worldview. It is generally best to make it clear that understanding the reasons behind an order is valuable, but being willing to obey regardless of understanding is more valuable.

Another good point to impress upon the ASD s-type is the concept of "right versus effective". If their goal is to ensure you have the flattest pants possible, then being a pedantic ass about it is not furthering their goal. What would be effective? Looking at things from another person's perspective is very challenging for many ASD folks, but it is a skill that can be learned and applied mechanically. It can be helpful if you can figure out how to explicitly state your priorities in a way that the s-type can see how, given those priorities, your choice is logically consistent. From there, they may be able to generalize surprisingly accurately, even if your priorities are very different from theirs.

Switching Gears

Raven: Have I mentioned yet that people with ASD don't like change much? That includes hour-to-hour changes. I'm a versatile master with a lot of different needs. Sometimes I want a quiet, efficient sidekick who will follow my instructions in the moment to the letter. Sometimes I want an intelligent, problem-solving sidekick who will brainstorm effective methods for a project with me. Sometimes I want a warm, supportive partner who will talk to me about emotionally intimate things, remaining respectful and loving at all times. Sometimes I want someone to hold me when I'm wracked with pain and at the end of my own resources. Sometimes I want an eager servant who wants nothing more than to give me pleasure, and glows at my compliment or orgasm. Sometimes I want a completely surrendered slave who trembles at my touch and desperately wants to spread himself vulnerably for me.

Joshua wants very much to be able to give me every one of those things, and he has. The problems inherent in that versatility, however, are twofold. First, although by the time I got him he'd already figured out how to act out some of those roles, there were others that he had no clue about, and I had to train him very specifically. "When I do this, you do that. When I am like this, you do that. When I indicate that I want this—in one of these three ways—then you do it in this way." While I'm not on the spectrum, I'm also not a very emotionally-oriented person—and, being a "control enthusiast" as a friend of mine put it, I can find pleasure in "programming" my slave to act in exactly the way I want, when I want it. I just have to be willing to put in the clear, precise work to do it. I also need to have a good understanding that for him, these "artificially trained" affects are not him slapping on an alien mask over his natural way of expressing; it's that he doesn't have a natural way of expressing them, and he might as well use one that pleases me. (He'll talk more about that further on. He's one of the less emotionally expressive sorts, in case you hadn't figured that out by now.)

Second, I have to make it very clear to him which sort of "slave role" I want from him, and for best results I need to let him know at least half an hour beforehand. For the more "intense" roles, it's best if he has an hour or thereabouts to himself, to get his head switched over to the affect and body language and emotional responses that I want from him. This takes time and effort for him; switching gears doesn't come quickly or easily. If I ask him to go into a mode of total surrender straight from coming home from work or playing an engrossing video game, he will become flustered and distressed, and be unable to give that to me. By giving him advance warning, I don't set him up for failure. This does cut down on a certain amount of spontaneity, but it's a compromise I am willing to make in order to get what I want. (If constant emotional and situational spontaneity was a very high priority for me in a M/s relationship, perhaps a slave on the spectrum wouldn't be the best choice. That's just a matter of being realistic about what you want before you get stuck together.)

Joshua: I often feel like my inner pressure cooker of emotions has no vent. I can feel like I'm full of emotions—I feel my body doing something—but the things that neurotypical people do to vent and express those emotions don't work. My emotions don't make the connection. For example, let's say that I think I may be sad right now. What do "ordinary" people do when they're sad? Well, they cry. Let me try to cry. No, this isn't helping, it doesn't connect to that emotion at all. It would be as if someone neurotypical was sad and I suggested that they lick their nose to feel better. Over time I've been able to program or condition myself into having my emotions connect to some activities, but really, it's all artificial for me. So I might as well condition actions that my master likes.

Where it's especially hard for him is that my behavior and the apparent intensity of my emotions may have little to do with the intensity of my internal emotional experience, so he can't make assumptions based on my body language and affect. I will inadvertently act as if I feel strongly about something when I don't, or not have much affect when I'm actually experiencing very intense emotions. It's up to me to communicate it verbally, because I know that I'm not giving clear nonverbal signals. Any relationship that didn't have a lot of radical honesty about emotions wouldn't work for me. If a partner did the "Oh, nothing's wrong," thing, I'd never catch on. I also need my master to trust that I'm giving him truthful information about my current state, so I'm careful when I communicate that in words.

I can't speak for anyone else but me here, but for me, being deeply surrendered and having problem-solving skills are two opposing states. When I'm in a state of emotional vulnerability and deep surrender, I panic when asked to do anything that requires more than a trivial amount of cognitive thinking. It's terrifying to follow any but the simplest and clearest of single-step orders, or established protocol that I've done so many times I could do them in my sleep. Being asked for my opinion or preferences in that state is also panic-inducing, because I lose them when I go there. It's also hard for me to keep my affect going—you'd be surprised how much work an expressive affect is for us—and that surrendered state comes with a purity of single-minded emotion that uses up all the resources I would normally use for facial expressions and body language. If I have to solve a problem or figure out an order, I have to come out of that space and go into "work mode".

I find that state very calming and fulfilling, but I realize that perversely, it's not all that much fun for my master, unless he's only interested in a warm body to do things to. I love being in a mindless, robotic state, but it's really not his kink. We still hold out hope that we can find a mutually fulfilling activity that can be done in that state, because it's no fun for either of us if he's doing something just to humor me.

Social Skills

Raven: Another classic hallmark of ASD is difficulty with socializing. Their neurological wiring is flawed when it comes to mentally interpreting people's clues of body language, facial expression, tone of voice, clothing choices, phrasing, etc. Understanding and utilizing those clues themselves, to communicate with others, is also not an option. Neurotypical people learn this unconsciously in childhood, because our brains are wired to do so, but folks on the spectrum don't have the same wiring. This leaves many of them feeling as if they are aliens, attempting to figure out some telepathic language that everyone else is speaking, and expecting them to speak as well. That's why they are often referred to as "dorky", "geeky", "weird", and sometimes "creepy" from people who are put off or made uncomfortable by their unusual behavior.

Some of them, however, have applied themselves to learning this alien language well enough to more-or-less understand and use it, because it can be learned intellectually, studied like one would study Japanese or Swahili. (Of course, it would be much simpler for them if there was actual instruction available as easily as taking a class in Japanese, but society isn't quite there yet.) They "pass" as normal, if perhaps slightly stilted or reserved or "old-fashioned", and can even be charismatic. What we don't see is that it costs them a great deal of focus and energy, and they can't do it 24/7, or perhaps even 12/7. Joshua has learned, painfully, a lot of good observation and social-affect skills, and most people think that he's charming when he's out with me (or at least "charmingly dorky"), but I know what that constant consciousness of body motions, tone of voice, and word choice is costing him. I know that he can't keep it up on a round of involved public social interactions, starting in the morning and ending in the wee hours, with no breaks.

That noted, I would not set him up for failure in this way, and I always assume for periods of rest and down time for him during public event weekends. (The fact that I have a second boy now is a great relief for him; if he's in no shape to go to a public party after a whole day of loud events where he is expected to be socially smooth, I can always take the other boy.) One hallmark of many folks on the spectrum—including high-functioning ones who are just having a hard day—is the loud, flat staccato voice with no apparent affect. When that voice starts coming out of Joshua, I know that he is "all out of charming", as he puts it, and needs to go be alone for a while.

I also accept that one of my jobs is to brief him on acceptable behavior in new or non-standard venues, and to stop him (often with coded pre-chosen verbal or gestural cues) if his behavior becomes unacceptable. On a less skillful or more overstimulated day, he might back someone into a corner while monologuing about some obsessive interest of his, not noting their desperate, fixed smile that (clearly only to someone neurotypical) longs to get away. It's my job to step in at that point and break up the interaction in some face-saving way for everyone, and then carefully go over it later so that we can figure out if there was any way he could have noticed. Sometimes there isn't, especially when he doesn't have enough resources on line to be aware of it; at that point, we talk about ways to head that state off at the pass.

Joshua: It is incredibly embarrassing for me to misjudge social circumstances, or say something that ends up being hurtful, or corner someone to babble endlessly at them about something I genuinely but mistakenly thought they had expressed interest in. I strongly prefer both that my master cue me about my behavior, and that he do it subtly so as not to embarrass me further. It's also more practical that way, because I don't want people making excuses for my inappropriate behavior. I'd rather just behave appropriately.

The idea of formal protocol—a well-defined set of behaviors—had great appeal for me when I got into M/s. I liked the idea that I could be told exactly what to do or say, and if I misstepped, it would immediately be explained and corrected. Sadly, my master is not very interested in formal protocol (which often seems to be submissive-driven in many cases, from what I've seen). A very formal situation with strict manners, where people are not allowed to act casually and do what they like, is—once I know the rules—actually much easier for me. It's the casual socializing that is hard for me, because the wider range of acceptable behaviors makes it harder for me to guess what not to do.

Early on in our relationship, my master made a rule that aside from a few specific friends, I was not allowed to touch women (and yes, he had to then clarify that sniffing them or sitting too close counted), especially in casual, touchy, flirtatious social situations. The problem wasn't that I was making awkwardly inappropriate attempts to flirt with women (I prefer older men sexually), but even affectionate touching from a man is a loaded minefield. It was very easy for me to misjudge what kind of physical contact was acceptable in those situations, and when I was younger I did some very inappropriate things. While those were innocent mistakes on my part, they were entirely unacceptable, so the safest course of action for me was to cope with being seen as a little uptight, as opposed to being freer with people and risking someone feeling violated because of our interaction.

Because I need to pay so much more attention to social rules (or risk being wildly inappropriate), I end up being very uncomfortable seeing my master violate social rules, even though I know that he's much more skillful at assessing that risk than I am. I also become uncomfortable when he puts me in situations where I am on the edge of risking social deviance. My fears make my social behavior limits much more conservative. Some people like to say, "I don't care what people think," but if I thought that way, I'd have no friends, no job, and no master. Me in my natural state just doesn't work in the world (although my master is OK with it to a certain extent in private with him). My master is one of those people who doesn't care what others think of him, but he knows how to maneuver on that edge. I don't have the skill to find that middle ground, and even though I know he's good at it, it still makes me nervous.

Structure and Rules

Raven: This, again, will vary depending on your ASD type. Some love and crave structure and rules, some don't. My slaveboy craves it so much that he's considered going into a monastery, except that he wasn't actually practicing the religion of the monasteries he'd gazed at longingly. (And he likes sex an awful lot, and he's queer, and ... anyway.) I wasn't structured enough for him—he longed for a micromanaging dominant who would keep him on a strict, unchanging schedule. Instead, he got me, and he copes as well as he can.

When I've spoken to s-types on the spectrum in the past, a majority of them spoke about how they loved the narrow, structured life of slavery. Rules gave them comfort, unlike ambiguous social and life situations where they are expected to guess ... and guess wrong all too often. Many also lauded the state of having one's basic decisions made for one—what to wear, how to walk, how to keep one's hair and nails, what to say to please their partner. Figuring those things out by themselves, often on the fly, was stressful enough that they would rather give up their choices and lay the decisions on someone else. (I remember Joshua's pleasure when I got him "uniforms" and told him what situations were acceptable for which ones; it meant that he would never again have to navigate the "What clothing is appropriate for this party/work/social occasion? I have no idea!" nightmare.) If they can learn to enjoy the emotional state of surrender (or already enjoy it quite a bit, thank you very much), this love of rules and structure can make them much more obedient than many other subs or slaves.

Of course, not all masters live lives of strict discipline, and order—I certainly don't—but giving him rules and protocols makes him feel secure, not restricted. That's definitely a plus in my book, and it makes for an exceptionally obedient slave. Other masters have commented wonderingly on how absolutely obedient he is; I smile and wonder how to tell them that his well-behaved rule-following probably has a lot less to do with my power as a master than his ASD-induced love of following rules.

One of the fundamental desires of any s-type is to clearly know what is expected of them in order to do their job correctly. Vagueness and inconsistency in this area can upset any of them, but for a sub or slave with ASD it is downright terrifying. It's more than a desire for them; it's a deep need, and one that a master shoots themselves in the foot by deliberately undercutting. On the positive side, though, I've found that unless they are also carrying a heavy burden of old PTSD and/or have an additional untreated neurochemical mental illness, most s-types with ASD are very good at taking constructive criticism in a positive way, especially if it is given in an emotionally neutral way (and they believe they have the ability to eventually succeed at it). Once they've been assured that it is simply an assessment and not an attack, they will usually be able to calmly take it as such, and work with it. That's another very positive side effect that masters may enjoy.

Joshua: I would love having one of those masters who wants you to put a specific number of ice cubes in his glass, and insisted the table be set with utensils carefully aligned exactly one inch from the table edge. That would make me so happy! I dreamed about having one who would put me through all sorts of formal protocol, and my challenge would be to master that discipline. Instead I have a master who is training me in how to be kind, loving, respectful, and skillful at social situations, as much as possible. It wasn't what I expected at all, but I am so much better for it. These skills are more difficult, because they are softer, but because of this, I can now teach in public as his co-presenter and hold down a career requiring a lot of people skills.

Emotional Expression

Raven: As we've mentioned, folks with ASD come in a variety of abilities to notice and identify their own emotions and express those in a socially acceptable way. Some of them, when behaving naturally, tend to express them in odd physical ways—hand-flapping, jumping up and down, making strings of strange noises, etc. Usually they've been discouraged from doing this in childhood, but it may still remain their favorite—if private—form of expression. Allowing them to indulge in it when you are alone together can be a great gift—you'll be the one person with whom they can be themselves.

Others don't seem to have any natural way to express emotion. (At its most severe, this is called *alexithymia*, which indicates a serious inability to feel or express emotions.) Joshua had trouble figuring out what he was feeling, so we worked on his awareness of his physical reactions; usually his stomach will figure out that he is stressed well before he does, if he ever does, so checking with his body helped a lot. (I later discovered that this is a therapy technique used for mild alexithymia.) It's not that he doesn't have emotions, it's that they don't have a natural way out. Someone like this could actually be a positive project for a master who enjoys shaping and controlling their s-type, as they could train them to consciously respond a certain way when they are feeling a certain emotion. Eventually the learned behavior would become the "doorway", and then you have a slave whose emotional reactions you've custom-designed. (That's what we're working on, slowly, over time. Such projects, of course, need to be entered into with the enthusiasm of the s-type, without whose aid you will not be able to achieve anything.)

Aside from that, if you really don't care that your s-type's response to happiness is to flap, beep, or just stand there like an expressionless statue, then it really doesn't matter. As long as they can verbalize their feelings enough to keep you in the loop, then things will be all right. Transparency may be a serious discipline for them, though, if only because it requires noticing, interpreting, and articulating feelings on a regular basis.

Joshua: It was incredibly freeing to understand my ASD diagnosis, and give myself "permission" to use ASD-type coping mechanisms in private. I'd already run through all the "normal" social expressions of those emotions, and even some of the pathological and unhealthy ones, as an attempt to make a connection between feelings and actions. I was so desperate to find behaviors that would connect meaningfully to my emotions that I intentionally tried a various self-harm behaviors, to see if that would work. (They didn't, fortunately.) However, when I finally got comfortable with my diagnosis, I tried some of the "traditional" ASD behaviors—hand-flapping, rocking, making high-pitched noises—and I was shocked by how good they felt, and how naturally they connected to my emotions. There really is some kind of neurological basis to those behaviors. Most of them are not appropriate in public, but it's great for me to have a new variety of coping behaviors (if only in private) to work with.

Self-Help and Resources

Raven: In general, the more that your s-type with ASD learns about their disorder and how it functions—which does mean learning enough about how neurotypical people work to understand the contrast—the more information they will be able to give you, and the more skillfully you'll be able to manage them. Therapy with a professional skilled in helping folks with ASD may help. For both of you, I suggest talking to other people on the spectrum, and especially other s-types on the spectrum if you can find them. They may have coping mechanisms that neither of you have thought of.

If your new s-type has given up on learning more—if they have become demoralized by their failure to figure it all out on their own, and decided that it's all just too confusing—remind them that Knowledge Is Power. The more they know about their own mind, the minds of others, and the contrast between them, the more opportunity they will have to create compensatory mechanisms and get more of what they want out of life.

Joshua: Unfortunately, a lot of the resources available are for parents or educators of children with ASD, and many seem excessively concerned with drilling the child in "normal" behavior, without understanding the reasons behind their unusual behavior. I recall an essay by one mother who, after years of scolding her son to have "quiet hands", tearfully realized that this was actually a way he expressed emotion, and that she had spent much of his childhood telling him, basically, not to do his equivalent of laughing or crying or expressing any feelings at all.

There is definitely great value in learning how to be socially appropriate, but for me to do that healthily, I had to come to it not from a place of self-hatred or hating everyone else's opaque behavior. A straight-up focus on drilling someone to be "normal" can be very demoralizing. It's important for you to look at their behaviors and decide which ones are completely inappropriate and which ones are just unusual, and while those latter ones may be slightly problematic in some situations, seriously consider whether they can be left alone as an expression of your s-type's individuality. If you don't understand your s-type well enough to see why they do all the weird things that they do, they will never trust you enough to allow you to train them.

Another thing to keep in mind is a point made by Temple Grandin: For many people on the spectrum, the most fulfilling thing in their life is not their social or relationship contact, but having meaningful work in their lives. This means that if it's handled right, a M/s relationship can be a truly amazing gift for them, especially if it is less about "having a relationship" (although it is certainly that) and more about "having the best job ever". It doesn't even matter if it is work that the world values, so long as they are good at it, enjoy it and find it fulfilling, and their master is pleased by it. For me, whatever other work I may do, this is my primary job—being Raven's slaveboy— and the me-that-I-was before I met him would never have believed how terrifically fulfilling this job can be. I've got a purpose in my life, and the best master ever. How much more lucky can one boy be?

Kajira with Autism

Hi, I'm Momo! I am a kajira (a Gorean slave girl) and the property of my Owner. We have a total authority transfer (otherwise known as TAT), blanket consent (or CNC as commonly known), Owner and property relationship. We are also Husband and wife. When we married, the word "obey" was left in my vows to him, and they were vows that I took very seriously, and continue to take very seriously 7 years later. He's the first and only Man that I have ever loved and I am proud to serve him, be his, and give my all to him.

As an autistic person, it can be incredibly hard for me to fit into the world around me; it often feels like operating in the world is one of those children's toys where you match the shape to the correct hole, but I'm a little fuzzy penguin, just waddling around without the tools to put the shapes into their respective holes ... because flippers and gross motor function don't mix.

In an ideal world, I would have access to a device that I could operate with my flippers or beak, something more penguin-friendly; I would be able to live in a world that I could easily fit into and function in and one where adaptations could be made so a little penguin such as myself could waddle and play and hunt and dance and slide and do other penguin things without being kept at a disadvantage, without being overwhelmed by everything around me, without being excluded, without being denied necessary resources ... but the world is not ideal.

For me personally, I am not wired to be in an egalitarian relationship (or a relationship where my partner and I share equality; equal rights, equal decision making, equal authority). Before I met my Owner and before I discovered my need to be a slave, I was a submissive and I had a part-time power exchange with a dominant, and this was horrible for me. My brain had a difficult time understanding the boundaries laid out of what he had power over and what he did not, as well as when I was supposed to be submissive and when I was not. The lack of consistency and structure that I needed created conflict between us, and I found myself feeling miserable and unfulfilled with regard to myself, and feeling a lack of respect for that dominant. He also did not understand what to do with an autistic person; when I would lose the ability to speak, he would accuse me of being manipulative and of trying to guilt him to get my way. He would yell at me, and when he changed plans on me, it made me feel as if I were a bad sub and a crazy person. When I tried to leave, he promised me things would change, but for another month they did not. It was more of the same: more inconsistencies, more yelling, and more confusion.

When I finally did leave, I was able to reflect on myself and I decided that being a submissive did not fulfill me; I needed more ... so much more. I needed something full-time and absolute; I needed structure, routine, consistency. I needed words to mean exactly what they said, I needed accountability, I needed to serve and devote myself to the person I would love. Being a kajira and being property is the most free that I have ever felt; I am free to be my authentic self, I am given structure and consistency that my brain needs, I am given clear expectations, I am held accountable for my words and behavior, and I am able to follow ... to follow expectations, to follow guidelines, to follow values, to follow Him.

In my relationship, I have no authority; I gave up my limits and safe words, and my right to leave. I also gave him blanket consent, meaning he no longer requires my OK to do things. I must seek his permission before spending any money on non-essential things that have been given approval already, and I am not permitted to spend more than $20 unless he says otherwise. And on the subject of money... he controls that. The money that I earn from work goes into our bank account; it is not my money ... it's his money. I have access to it for necessity but not for leisure spending without his permission. I have opinions and he welcomes my opinions, but I do not get a say. I also gave up my right to leave. I am his property, much like his car (but more valuable and more loved) and I have never been happier. For my brain, this is an ideal relationship; my Owner is very consistent, I have structure and routine, and I have clear expectations to follow that are always present.

I found surrendering to him to be the easiest thing I have ever done—it came naturally. With an egalitarian relationship, I would find myself in constant power struggles because I *need* leadership. It helps me function. I *need* to follow, to obey, to serve. I *need* structure and consistency and clear expectations. For me, obedience has never been an issue; if at times I struggle, I am given time to process and work myself up to doing whatever I am told to do. I am lucky that my Owner is not the type of Man to push things just because he can; for example, he has never taken a food that he knows I am unable to eat and ordered me to eat it, right then and there, immediately—*do it, go*. He has never done this. He may discover something that I am reluctant to do and I may have some pushback in the form of delay (never outright refusal), and when that happens he gives me time to process and get on the same page, and then I obey and do whatever it was he told me to do. I don't know what would happen if we discovered a serious hurdle where I struggled and fought him—we have not had that happen yet. I do know we would communicate, a lot. I think it would depend on the impact it was having on me; if something was causing a threat to my well-being, I don't foresee him pushing it on me.

Sometimes certain services are difficult for me. I used to make coffee by hand before we got a French press. I would scoop the beans into a hand-grinder and then turn the lever until all the beans were ground to the consistency that my Owner preferred. Then I would pour them into the filter and pour boiling water over them in slow, circular patterns, until a full cup of coffee was strained. This was particularly difficult for me, with my autism, because it involved repetitive fine motor movement, which I struggle with (same reason I can't knit). It often frustrated me, despite how much I loved doing it for him. There were a few times I simply didn't do it, and dealt with the consequences of that choice. For the most part, though, I did it because it was my task to do, and it was something that pleased him. I want more than anything to please him.

One service that my autism actually had a positive impact on was pouring his drinks! My Owner is a craft beer enthusiast; when in the military, he traveled all across the world and found favored beers in other countries. When I learned of this, I made beer a special interest of mine and I researched the heck out of it—specifically, how to properly pour it. I researched different types of beer, different types of glasses, which ones to use for which beers, how to properly pour beer into those specific glasses, and how to properly pour specific beers into specific glasses. That became an obsession for me, and it was something I took extraordinary pride in, and still do to this day. Other acts of service that are made easier because of my autism are laundry (I am particular about how things are cleaned, including that they are cleaned exceptionally well, and I am particular on how laundry is treated and folded) and anything to do with organization—tidiness and cleaning, keeping shopping lists and the calendar, etc. I am very, very structured and organized.

There is the issue of cooking, though. I'm not the best cook, and this is due to my autism and not an inability to cook. Growing up, I was very restricted as to what I would eat and not eat, due to sensory issues. This did not change as I got older and before I knew it, I was an adult who only knew how to cook a handful of very basic dishes, with very basic ingredients. My Owner is more of a culinary person than I am; he likes trying new food, he likes layered flavors, he likes various textures, he likes spices, and so forth. Basically, he likes everything that I don't ... and everything that I don't know how to cook. I was able to cook his favorite soup once, as a surprise—Tom Kha soup—and it came out pretty well. He was very pleased. Due to my lack of cooking experience and inability to taste the various things he would like to eat, he does most of the cooking. This is something that I struggle with, in our situation; I will often feel like a bad slave because my Owner has to cook. He consoles me and tells me that he doesn't mind, and he enjoys cooking (and I know he does; he enjoys it very much), but I still feel disappointed in myself, like I am letting him down. I try to offer to cook more, but he tells me no; I will still keep offering and I am working on trying to find recipes that he would like, to see if he will allow me to cook them for him.

Despite having a TAT relationship where he has all the authority and I have none, my autism acts as a separate entity, sometimes outside of both of our control. I have an app on my phone that I use where I can track different things each day and then look for patterns over time. This is super helpful for me to see what is having positive and negative effects on me. *If I have a meltdown, what factors contributed to it? Did it involve self-injury? If I had a really great day, what factors contributed to it?* Patterns are very important for me. Some things that happen that my Owner, despite all of his authority, cannot control. If I lose the ability to speak, him commanding me to speak doesn't make it magically happen. If I have a neurological meltdown and bang my head on the floor, my Owner commanding me to stop doesn't work. Even though my autism is very much part of me and part of who I am, it doesn't have a TAT relationship with my Owner. He's respectful of it and mindful of it, and he works with my autism to help me cope through difficulties and manage what I am able to manage. He waited five months to get me to try a new food and he waited six months for me to make partial, brief eye contact with him. No amount of command would have made those things happen any sooner, and it might have had an opposite impact—a detrimental one, where they would have taken much longer to come about. My Owner does not feel like he has no authority over me, or like my autism is Master of him; he simply feels like I have some special considerations and I require a different kind of approach, and a different kind of effort, than someone else.

I think people, in general, have limitations. Some people have physical limitations such as trouble with eyesight or hearing, heart conditions, issues with blood sugar, trouble with their knees or hands, etc. Some people have mental limitations such as depression or anxiety, bipolar disorder, schizophrenia, or in my case ... autism. My Owner doesn't feel like someone else's limitations—in this case, mine—diminish his authority. It's simply something he works with, as he would if I had any kind of physical limitation. He understands that it doesn't take away from my devotion, obedience, or service to him and that's what he cares the most about—the intent I have with regard to our relationship, and specifically the effort I put in to be the best kajira I can be, to serve him and please him, and fill his life with happiness.

For me, the world is a place that I live at odds with due largely in part to sensory issues; these are a very common challenge that people diagnosed with autism experience. Often, but not always, they are divided into one of two categories: Hypersensitivity and

Hyposensitivity. The former means that a person naturally receives too much sensory input (over-reactive): sounds are inherently louder, light is inherently brighter, smells can be more overpowering, and that person may experience extreme skin sensitivity and touch sensitivity. On the opposite end, hyposensitivity means that a person naturally receives too little sensory input (under-reactive): sounds are more dulled and quiet, light isn't as bright or vibrant, it can be difficult to detect and distinguish smells, and a person may have a significantly reduced pain tolerance due to having a difficult time feeling tactile sensory input (such as firm impact, burns, cuts, etc.).

I have hypersensitivity, so that is where I can share experiences. However, if you suspect that you experience hyposensitivity and are in need of support, I recommend seeking out a qualified and licensed mental health professional so that you can receive the proper assessments, diagnostic clarification, and access to the supports available for you based on your own individual experiences and needs, such as but not limited to: physical therapy, vision therapy, listening therapy, and if needed, speech and language therapy. You may also consider making modifications to your living environment and integrating (more minor) sensory stimuli to work on coping with these experiences.

The three primary areas where I struggle with sensory processing are visual, auditory, and tactile. I also have an auditory processing disorder which has an impact on my communication, as well. For me, sounds are naturally magnified; my brain will process normal speaking voices as people yelling, lights are often too bright, and my tactile sensitivity ranges from how food and liquids feel in my mouth, to how sensitive my skin is to hair and chemicals and clothing, to how I process physical touch. I want to touch on each of these individually so that I can talk about how I experience them and what things I do to help.

Visual sensitivity has to do with how my brain processes lights and colors, my depth perception processing, and how my brain processes everything that I see. A common expression used for people with autism who experience hypersensitivity is that we "have no filter" (in our brains); the average neurotypical person is able to filter out approximately 80% of stimuli that occur throughout their day, which is due to this "filter". Without that "filter", an autistic person who experiences hypersensitivity does not have the capability to "tune out" stimuli that they receive, be it visual or auditory or olfactory or tactile. Everything is received and everything must be processed. This can become incredibly overwhelming.

Lightbulbs can be too bright for me and cause pain in my eyes. Sunlight can be unbearable and force my eyes closed, sometimes taking fifteen minutes or longer before I can open them again. I'm prone to stumbling and bumping into things due to how my brain processes depth in coordination with where I am and my own motor function. I can also become overwhelmed by all of the visual stimuli that I process simultaneously; every detail, every moment, every color (included with all my other senses). Some things that I have personally found to be helpful are: blackout curtains, higher end sunglasses (category 3 or 4, or FL-41), and finding focal points to fixate on. When with my Owner, he becomes my focal point; I will look at him (even just his presence near me) to help me fixate on one thing as opposed to everything. When I am not with him, I find that listening to music or wearing noise-cancelling headphones helps because that minimizes one source of sensory input and allows me "more room" to manage the visual input. I also use hand fidgets that I will make a focal point, as well. In our home, we use fewer light bulbs and more "secondary" light sources such as "accessory lights" as opposed to main room ceiling lights. This helps keep my environment comfortable.

As I mentioned above, I have a pair of noise-cancelling headphones; these are not for music, but rather full ear protection, such as when one might dispense a firearm. They are comfortable and secure and most of all very effective. For me, my headphones are a life necessity and I do not leave the house without them. Just writing these words are going to cause a tremor for me, but: Car horns and emergency sirens. These things are the bane of my happiness and I have such a hard time dealing with them; there are no words in the English language to describe the physical pain these sounds cause me. Sounds, in general, have a huge physical impact on me, right down to my nerves. I tried to ask my Owner how to describe it, and I described it to him in my way, and he said, "Sometimes there aren't words to describe what you're trying to say." Maybe that can be telling on its own.

Sudden loud noises are likely to cause a meltdown for me. Other sounds can, also. Recently, my Owner was listening to a song and it consisted of a skit performance. The voice was robotic sounding, but in such a way as I have never heard before. I noticed that I was having a reaction; it wasn't a conscious experience. I started to twitch as well as jerk my head sideways; I covered my ears and asked to turn it off. He said he would get it but it was too late. I ran to the bedroom and got under my weighted blanket and started shaking and crying. It all hurt. The best way that I can describe it is that it felt like a cold, metallic rib-cage-shaped instrument, that fluctuated rapidly between liquid and solid, with sharp curves, being dragged slowly over my bones and my nerves. I cried and cried, finally calming myself by reciting my list of sharks over and over. Sharks are a special interest of mine. My Owner came in and laid with me and got me through it.

I mentioned that I have an auditory processing disorder. For me, this means that my brain will black out random words that people speak; I will hear the sounds, but not the words, and my brain won't process them (via translating them into pictures). It also means that I need extra processing time; I don't transition well from (something I am doing) to (person speaking to me) without time to shift my focus from one to the other. I'm rubbish at doing both, also. It helps me to have pauses with verbal direction and storytelling; telling me a little bit and then being quiet for a few moments while I process what was said. That also gives me time to communicate if I need more information. My Owner will begin to tell me something and then he waits a moment for me to confirm that I'm ready to hear more or he lets me communicate that I need him to repeat something or that I'm not sure what something means. This is very helpful for me. Our communication wasn't always the best; before either of us knew that I had an auditory processing disorder, he would just talk at me and tell me stories about things or recount his day and I would sit there, lost and confused because I missed things he said (despite hearing him and being focused on him) and I would just respond with, "Yeah."

That didn't make for good conversations, and it often left him feeling like I didn't care much about what he told me. Now that we have adjusted our communication style and he gives me more processing time, I'm able to follow along with him and participate in conversations more. I also use my noise-cancelling headphones whenever I leave the house and I keep them on me at all times; I highly, highly recommend them if you have auditory sensitivity. If you do get a pair, be sure to get one of the higher-end ones that block out more noise. (Mine are Peltor 3M and I recommend them with enthusiasm.) The next step above this particular model are the ones you use more frequently when discharging a firearm; those are too thick for me and not as comfortable, but your mileage may vary. Be wary of ones that work the same as earplugs; they are good for a "quiet library" setting, not active noise cancellation. The only other thing I can recommend is to have a self-soothing plan developed; have a quiet place that you can go if you need that quiet time, and have techniques that you can use to cope if you become overwhelmed and overstimulated.

The auditory processing disorder often results in my becoming frustrated from being unable to follow people's directions or story or joke, or whatever it was they said. My Owner helps me with this by pausing in places when he tells me things in order to give me time to process, as well as an opportunity to tell him that I didn't process a certain word (such as, "I didn't get what you said after 'hamburger'"). I heard the sounds of what he said, but they didn't become words in my brain, so I was unable to process them. This extra processing time is very helpful for me and makes it so I can participate more in conversations and understand what it is he tells me to do or shares with me (such as recounting his day or a story).

Tactile sensitivity refers to the things that we can physically feel. For me, this includes the texture of food and the sensation of liquid in my mouth (the temperature, the texture, the places it touches and how, the pressure), how I process physical touch, and skin sensitivity (hair on my body, how clothing feels, how laundry detergents and soaps and shampoos affect my skin, and so forth). I am incredibly restrictive when it comes to food that I eat; I am avoidant when it comes to anything new and I have a long, long list of food that I will not eat due to texture and taste. This particular issue has improved over the years with the help of my Owner, who slowly chipped away at the giant marble NOPE that was my food willingness. When we first met, it took him five months to get me to try a new food, but I eventually did and I liked it a lot. Over the years he's gotten me to try many new foods and broadened my culinary palate; some of the foods he's gotten me to try—and like—are: asparagus, cauliflower, carnitas, jalapenos, buttered chicken, pad thai, pad see ew, garlic, hummus, pesto, and beans. For me, this is a *lot* of new, but over the years he was patient and persistent. What helped most was incorporating these foods into dishes that I could—and would—eat. For example, wrapping a jalapeno in bacon and putting cheese in it made me more willing to try it because I would already eat both bacon and cheese. He also started small by making just one piece of something, or one bite, as opposed to an entire dish.

I use silverware designed for children (spoons and forks) because I have an aversion to metal and large objects in my mouth (yes, the exception to that is the dirty joke you may have just asked yourself, haha). I also use straws to assist with drinking liquids, as I hate the sensation of "open-floodgates" liquid pouring into my mouth (which I also tend to spill); straws help to regulate the liquids, keep them compact, and help them go from point A (straw) to point B (throat). Physical touch is more straightforward for me and less subject to conditions and modification; I cannot tolerate light physical touch sensations, such as fingertips or gentle tapping or even kisses—it makes me spazzy and stabby. I hate it. I prefer, and need, strong and forceful physical contact; I absolutely love deep pressure, and for our anniversary my Owner got me a 25-pound weighted blanket which has been such a help to me. I sleep under it every night, and when I feel overwhelmed I can go hide under it, and get that deep pressure sensation that I need. My Owner also helps because he will lay his full body weight on me at times if I ask or he will "smoosh" my head in his hands, which makes me very happy.

Something I have to be mindful of is other people touching me without my consent, which does happen. Often it's to get my attention; someone will come tap me on the arm. My natural instinct is to jerk away from them and rub/scratch the place that they touched while twisting and jerking my arm around, but this tends to offend people. To be honest, sometimes I just don't care; if doing that will help me, I'm going to do it. Other times I will try to restrain myself until I can go somewhere more private. Having that mindfulness is something that I work on; learning to cope with the things that happen sometimes so that I can respond appropriately, for myself and for the other person involved. That could even include me telling them, "Hey, I don't like to be touched." Whatever works for you.

With skin sensitivity, that requires more maintenance. I have an allergy to a chemical that is in most beauty products, so I have to read every label for shampoos, conditioners, body washes, soap, lotions, detergents, and make-up products. Luckily once you find things that work for you, the maintenance isn't as high; however, if you ever want to try new things, get anything professional done, or receive gifts from people... read those labels. I personally also need to be mindful of clothing that I wear; certain kinds of clothing will cause irritation to my skin and result in rashes and me scratching myself. I also cannot tolerate layers with clothing which often results in me wearing short-sleeves and a thin coat during the winter or long-sleeves and no coat during the winter. I usually also wear sandals until there's snow on the ground; my feet can only deal with the soft and fuzzy socks. For clothing, it's super important to find what works for you and your sensory sensitivities; this is often a trial and error until you discover what works best for you. Consider the texture, the fit, whether or not you have sensitivity to layering, and even how the clothing adapts to different elements like heat and cold and saturation. All of these things can impact your preferences.

So what happens when sensory input becomes overwhelming? Well, this is called overstimulation and it can lead to a meltdown. For me, meltdowns occur when I receive so much sensory input that my brain struggles to process all of it. It's like a gigantic tangle of differently colored strings, all of different lengths, all with different textures, and off of each dangles a small shape playing a different animation of something. Each animation is different—pixilated, clear, colors, sounds and no sounds, just hundreds upon hundreds of all of these moving things that intersect and intertwine. Someone with autism, with no filter, would see all of this at once—all this sensory stimulation that we can see, and hear, and smell, and physically feel. For me, when I have a meltdown, my brain is unable to process all of this sensory information; it lags, basically, but all the sensory information is still incoming—it never stops.

My brain will shut down and process everything that I am seeing, everything that I am hearing, and smelling and experiencing as raw, microscopic pain. I often describe it as my nerves being electrocuted and lit on the fire at the same time. Everything just hurts, my whole body seizes up and stiffens and I curl up and start screaming and crying. Depending on how bad it is, I may experience self-injury, as well where I will scratch and hit myself or bang my head on the wall or floor. This is not a conscious decision at the moment; it's a primal impulse that my brain sends to try and provide some kind of relief from all the pain. This is often when I lose my ability to speak and it can take up to an hour, or longer, to get it back.

When I have meltdowns, he removes expectations from me for a short while, to prevent further pile-on and stimulation, and in recognition that I am not in a place to meet them. I'm not given free rein to do whatever I want, of course, but he doesn't push me to use words when I'm unable to, and he exercises more patience with me as I work through the meltdown because it can be anywhere from one hour to several hours before I am able to speak again, and often several hours before I regain regulation of my pitch and tone. During that time, I communicate primarily with gestures and the use of a text to speech program on my phone. I have numerous necessary phrases stored there and it has a keyboard output for typing. When I am unable to speak, using it is tremendously helpful for things that I need to communicate where gestures just don't sufficiently convey those things.

In my relationship, my Owner is incredibly aware of my sensory needs. This past Christmas he got me two bubble bath sets, and when I opened them he immediately told me, "I read the label multiple times and didn't see any Dimethicone or silicates." He will buy me utensils that I can use—despite them being for children—instead of ones I "should" use. He doesn't want to buy clothes for me because I need to feel things first—I don't have a list of specific materials that are automatically good for me—but when I find things that I do like and can wear, he gives me his approval and permission (or not) to get it. When I have meltdowns, he sits with me and ensures I'm safe while giving me whatever I need in the moment (this could be quiet or back rubs or my fidgets or a firm hug).

The most important thing for me, for him, and for us is communication. My Owner can't experience these things for me or take them away from me, and he can't be there for me and help me, unless I communicate my experiences and needs to him. Sometimes he can't relate to them and sometimes he can't fully understand them, but other times he sees where I am coming from. At all times, though, he does his best to support me and be there for me.

I think that's the best "accommodation" I have ever received, because before him, no one did that for me. No one took the time to learn about me or understand me. He was the first. He was the first of so many things for me, the first and only, and that's one reason I love him so much and one reason I have been able to accept myself for who I am is because he did it first.

Communication can be a challenge when it comes to autism, both for the person who is autistic and the person—or people—in a relationship with them. I'm autistic and for me, my challenges are many; sometimes the challenge is translating the pictures in my head into words that I can say, other times the challenge is keeping words separated when I speak to avoid them blending together into a different and nonsensical word. Sometimes it's not being able to find any words for what it is I am trying to express. Occasionally the challenge is that I lose my ability to verbally communicate at all, which is called *apraxia of speech*, or AOS. This is a speech sound disorder that has many, many effects on my verbal communication and has been present for my whole life. When I experience meltdowns, it's what causes my physical inability to speak; I am unable to take sounds and turn them into syllables, and then those into words, and those words into sentences.

Communicating has always been a struggle for me, moreso when I was a child, but it continues to be something that requires a great deal of effort on my part now as an adult. My Owner does not experience any sort of communication impairments and so our communication styles differ greatly; while he prefers to verbally communicate and discuss, I prefer the use of sounds, hand flapping, gestures, and words that are more natural for me to speak, which are not always grammatically correct or even actual words, in certain cases. We have had to learn to accommodate each other over the years; him with learning my style of communication and me with putting in the effort to speak more when I am able and taking the time to process my thoughts so that I can find the words to express them to him.

Balance is important in our relationship, and we find it by meeting each other where we can. For example, some days it may be easier for me to verbally communicate and I might speak more (perhaps with correct word use and with incorrect word use, but I am still communicating). Other days I might be overstimulated and only able to say "frupplefo!" while flapping my hands, and although my Owner doesn't know what a "frupplefo" is, he understands the frustration I am expressing and understands that I am frustrated and unhappy about something that happened in my day. He might ask me leading questions to help me focus and use more sounds, as I personally respond very well to leading questions. Instead of asking me who or what this is, or what specifically took place, he will ask me: Is this a person? Did something happen at work? Did something happen at your appointment? Questions which are "yes or no" help to narrow down what I am trying to express. This helps my brain to focus and sort through the pictures in my head better so that maybe, at some point, I can respond with, "My routine," which would be a more specific (and helpful) word use. As he works with me, I'm usually able to find more words and then build sentences with them.

As you can see, my Owner accommodates a lot with me and sometimes that balance isn't even; sometimes I need more accommodation than he does and that's something I struggle with. I struggle to accept that and be okay with it; I struggle to not feel like a burden to him and I struggle to not beat myself up for messing up my words or missing things that he says or being unable to talk with him at times. I remember, though, that I am doing what he asks of me—I am trying my best. Some days are better than others and I do a great job communicating my needs in a way that is more natural for him—just simply telling him, using words. Some days the challenge impacts me more and I have a harder time, but I do my best. We often use text throughout the day when we are apart, and that helps us both.

Ours is a relationship where he cannot command my autism away, nor would he try. We both put the effort in to meet in the middle; him with being more patient and understanding, and learning my kind of preferred communication, and me with working on verbal communication more, writing him notes, and using my text to speech program. He's worked with me a great amount over the years to help me get to a place where I am less hard on myself and more accepting of who I am so that I can be more accepting of his love and Ownership of me. The best thing I can do is be transparent with him, ask for help when I need it, and do my best when it comes to communicating, that's all he really demands of me. And I can do that—for me, for him, and for us.

In closing, a hopeful-advice-offering. If you are an M-type and you are considering a relationship with someone who is autistic, I beg you to understand that we are all different. If you know one person with autism, you only know one person with autism. The best person to tell you what your s-type needs is them; listen to them and be open with them. Ask about their wants and needs and be honest and realistic, both with them and yourself. If you cannot meet their needs or feel they cannot meet yours, there is no shame in that. People can be incompatible for many reasons and sometimes that reason may be that you aren't able or willing to provide what that s-type needs. That is okay. The best thing you can do is be honest and up-front about that to prevent future conflict and disharmony. I think it's important to always be realistic—autism is *not* a disease and does *not* need to be treated like it should be cured. Embrace your partner for who they are, quirks and all.

If you are an s-type with autism, do your best to develop and maintain healthy boundaries while you get to know potential M-types. Think about what you want and need from a potential partner and your relationship, and make sure you don't settle for anything less. Be sure to be open and honest with any potential partners about who you are and what you need. Also be accountable to yourself; take care of yourself, learn how to cope with things that may go poorly, practice navigating social situations, and manage what you can manage. Your experiences are valid and your feelings are valid. Unless you consent otherwise, never let anyone put you down or try to change you. You are perfect as you are.

For both: communicate, communicate, communicate. Communication is fundamental. Remember the big picture and put in the effect to consistently be on it—together.

Signed, a very happy and lucky, autistic little penguin.

Momo is a kajira who has been happily owned by MDB for 9 years. They met through mutual acquaintances and the rest was history. Momo and MDB live with their two cats in a small house and a larger garden. Momo enjoys painting, writing and pleasing her Owner. Power exchange has been a life changing experience for her; the structure and routine and consistency that her Owner and relationship provide has helped her grow and flourish. Being an s-type is her nature and being with MDB has taught her to embrace who she is and live as her authentic self.

Interview with Bella and Ty

Bella: We're Bella and Ty, and we're an M/s couple. We've been together for eight years now, almost nine, and we've been in an authority transfer relationship the entire time. Once we did our contract signing and collaring, I gave him authority over everything in my life.

My autism has definitely been hanging around for a long time, since I was very little. I have a hard time with having clear boundaries with other people, and I have a lot of sensory issues as well. My brain sometimes feels like a little bouncy squirrel, and it really needs to be in a box in order to feel like it knows what to do. Within the boundaries of the box, everything is free rein, but outside of the box it feels like constant choice paralysis about my whole life. The autism wasn't something that we knew about until about two years ago, because I was never diagnosed as a child. It's been a new thing for us to be able to take a lot of my difficulties and turn them into ... well, if not positives, then at least not negatives. The knowledge has made them manageable.

Ty: I don't look at Bella's autism so much as a diagnosis as a set of behaviors, which we now know fall into these categories. Some of them were difficult but manageable, and then there were others that were ... well, weirder—but I really like them! For example, the fact that there's never any subtext to read with her communication. Ever. She says exactly what she means, and she means what she says, and that is consistent. It is not always easy or pleasant—although she's gotten better at that over the years—but it is something that I learned very early to rely on and appreciate, and I kind of wish the rest of the world was more like that, honestly.

What comes with that, though, is that as someone on the top side of the relationship, you need to really have your ego in check to be able to handle this. I think there are a lot of people on the left side of the slash who don't have that balance, and who see this behavior as an affront, or as a challenge, when it's really just taking off bullshit social guises and getting down to the root of the matter.

Bella: People do weird little dances with their communication, when they don't have that straightforwardness, and I always find that bizarre. I'm still learning how to deal with that. I've gotten better about it over the years, because your mom is very WASPy, and I've had to learn that like a strange language. But it is nice that you don't have a problem with me just opening my mouth and blurting out things.

Ty: I love it. It's amazing. And I think it's good for her to have a reprieve from that in our relationship, where it's not something she has to modulate, or has to think about other people's subtexts. I think that makes her a happier person.

Bella: Well, it makes it a lot easier for me, honestly, because I don't have to worry about constantly making sure that my voice has specific emotional inflections, or that my face has the right feelings showing on it. Because when left to my own devices, it's just my face, but people have problems with the way I look. The "tone" of my face is wrong. And it is nice to not have to worry about that at home.

We've had some difficulties with me going out of the house, though. When I'm going to places which have a lot of overstimulation—like Costco, for example—where I can hear all the lights and electricity running, and all the people are everywhere, that's really hard for me. Which means that it was really hard for *us*, for a long time.

Ty: We've worked out mitigating solutions that work really well. For example, she has earplugs which don't cancel out all sound—they're subtle and they sort of muffle everything—and over the years we've gotten really good at being able to communicate with hand signals, so we can negotiate something like a Costco trip completely nonverbally, which is great.

Bella: If he's standing close enough to me—no-more than a few feet away—I can hear him, but it blocks out all the extraneous stuff that ends up overwhelming me. That's helped me a lot, because I was having meltdowns. It had become so difficult, and I would get so anxious even before going into that. But once we started figuring out ways to block things out, it made it so much easier in so many different ways.

Ty: Because we don't have an egalitarian relationship, she doesn't get to decide which ideas she wants to try or not try or is comfortable with, which is good because she won't always try to help herself. I make sure that she has set tasks to do in that framework which will help focus her and get her through the situation. So our M/s relationship helps manage those things for her in an emotionally better way.

Another example of her overstimulation issues is with public scenes in dungeons. The fact that I can take away any need for her to negotiate with other people—and by that I mean social exchange negotiation out of scene—or taking away people's judgment around how she's responding to things, that's helpful. Often people have expectations around someone who just got the shit beat out of them— how they should respond, how they should be feeling, what expressions they should have, and she doesn't match a lot of those expectations.

Bella: They keep trying to shove cookies at you. It's terrible.

Ty: So my having oversight over that really helps. But knowing that she's really consistent with that means that I don't have to second-guess myself. If she says, "I'm good, I'm fine," then I don't need to assess that, or wonder if she's really fine or not. I don't have to play any of those games, which is fantastic.

Bella: He runs interference with other people afterwards, because at that point I don't have the spoons to keep my "face tone" acceptable. Sometimes it's just easier for him to say, "She's not talking right now." And I just get to sit there and be quiet, which is actually really nice.

Ty: For me, not having a partner who insists on those WASPy social graces is a relief – I don't have to deal with that in my home. But one of the ways in which I exploit her nature is that she's really good at making phone calls for me that I don't want to deal with, like dealing with a bill or negotiating the unpleasantness with the dryer installation. Because she doesn't take it personally, and she deals with the frustrating nature of it matter-of-factly, she manages it very well. I certainly take advantage of that; I sometimes refer to it as "letting her off her leash".

Bella: It helps that I'm really good with repetitive things. For example, when you're trying to deal with a medical referral and you're talking to seventeen different people, it's "And now I need your name. And then I'd like your birth date. And now I need to know about blah blah blah." And when you need to say that seven times in one phone call, a lot of people get frustrated with it, but it doesn't feel problematic to me. It's just what the path is.

Having really specific rules about things can be difficult in its own right if I feel like I'm going to have trouble living up to them. But a lot of what we do is more of an all-encompassing situation where he knows how he wants things, and I imitate that. Sometimes it takes a while to figure out how to imitate that most efficiently.

Ty: It can take years to figure out the methodology to get someone to do things the way you want them to do it. It's a cyclical process of finding out what works where. But in a lot of ways, her being on the spectrum has helped, because I don't have to dance around those rules. I don't even always have to tell her why I want this in a certain way. It's just "This is the right way," and she's just really good at just accepting that. I don't find that a lot in the world outside the spectrum.

I say this as someone who works professionally with engineers, many of whom do fall on the spectrum, and I find them very refreshing. They don't need the sociological backstory, they just say, "You want it to look like this? OK."

Bella: I have difficulty with long lists of rules, because the memorization aspect of it adds its own weird anxiety. What if I forget now that I have this twenty-ninth rule added on? But with our contract, we did it as more of an overarching thing. I'm just expected to make everything accessible, and that feels a lot easier than having to remember very specific protocols. Which we do have, in some ways, but we brought them in over time. It wasn't like a list of presented rules. Over time he would just say, "No, this needs to be more over here," and I would adjust myself in that regard.

Ty: I've learned to parse things out smaller, in more manageable steps. As each of those things becomes integrated with her, and move into her muscle memory, then we can move to the next little thing, which I will present in smaller chunks.

There are certainly parts of her autism which need to be managed; things I can't take for granted, and which require me to use a little more intelligence in how I assign things, or how I expect tasks to be done. For example, at the beginning I couldn't just say, "Clean the kitchen." I had to explain what that entails. So it required a little more work on my part to parse things out, and play with different methods—"Will this work? Will this work instead? Something's off here, how can I adjust?" I have to buffer things when it comes to our social life. I'm very introverted myself, so not having much of one isn't a problem, though. To a certain extent I design our lives to cope with her sensory issues.

Bella: As I've said, one of our biggest problems is that once we get into a space that's too overstimulating and noisy, which might feel normal or exciting to other people, it makes it really difficult for me to focus on any one thing at a time. So sometimes even something like making sure to follow behind him when he's walking somewhere can be difficult.

Ty: So we've come up with little ways to compensate, like "Grab my belt loop and stay on it." It's not that these are so much negatives as that they do take additional time, planning, and the ability—and willingness—to adapt quickly. If we get into the middle of a situation and it becomes unmanageable and we need to change course, that's OK.

Bella: And I've become much better at conveying to you when I'm starting to have those issues. That was really difficult at first!

Ty: Before we knew about all this, and had more tools in our toolbox to understand what was happening, we'd get into situations which were well past what she could handle. From my perspective, as someone who is not on the spectrum, at first everything was all right and then suddenly things were completely unmanageable. We spent quite a few years figuring out the "pre-symptoms" before things really started to break down with her, so that we could make adjustments there rather than down the road. That was a pretty big win for us, actually.

Bella: I'm not very good with enteroception, so recognizing when my body is hungry or cold is difficult. I'll just sit there and be cold, and it doesn't occur to me to get up and get a blanket. It was hard for me to recognize when those feelings were happening, and so I would end up pushing past my "I'm super hungry and haven't had a moment to rest" situation.

Ty: That's a place where our M/s comes in really handy, though. Now that I know where a lot of those points are, I can tell when she hasn't eaten and she's losing her mind, and I can say, "You need to eat now," or "You need to step away and take a nap," or "Drop it. Go somewhere else." She doesn't do that on her own very well.

Bella: His insistence there made it easier for me to see these crucial points, so I've gotten better at recognizing when I'm hungry, or even just saying, "I don't feel well. There's something wrong."

Ty: I think that it was by Year Two or Three I learned that if she says, "I could eat in the next hour or so," that means she's probably five minutes behind the time when she should have eaten, and if I don't deal with it now, it's going to snowball, and make it more difficult for her to do everything else.

Bella: It's one thing to have a partner say, "Oh, do you think you're hungry?" and I respond with, "No, I have seventeen other things I have to finish, and I've got two hours to do it," versus a partner saying, "No. You need to stop what you're doing and go eat lunch." That made a big difference, because I ended up learning that this need is a real thing. Hunger and exhaustion are real things. It helped that he would say, "I notice that you doing this thing right before you get to the point of melting down." That helps me to look out for that signal. We're still figuring it out and fine-tuning it, because it's been eight years and while it's improved, it's still not right. If we're out and about, doing a long day of errands, letting him know that "I think there's something going on. I think I might be hungry. You said that I do this when this is happening, and that's happening!" gives him the information he needs to make a decision about what I should do.

I have some issues with physical touch, although that's mostly around emotional distance from people. I will not seek it out. Even if I'm thinking, "Oh, yeah, it would be nice if somebody touched me," it doesn't occur to me to move over and touch him, or do the things I think people normally do when they feel cuddly. I think cuddling, in general, is very different for me than it is for most people. I'm pretty happy to just have my foot touching someone and call that a really solid cuddle. A lot of people apparently do not feel that is how cuddling should be! So I'm often not as physically affectionate as I probably could be. I need to make a specific point of thinking, "Oh, this is probably a time when I should be touching him."

Ty: I've also gotten pretty good at asking for what I want or need. Should I be in the mood for, say, cuddles, I will be very specific about what I need at that time, and very rarely, if ever, is that something she's unable to give. Now I don't think that applies to outsiders. There are certainly times when we're out, and I know that she's in a "no contact with other people" space, so I will hold that boundary and say, "No, she's not talking, or hugging, or shaking hands with anyone tonight." I just take that off the table as an option for her.

Bella: It feels nice to me that I don't have to worry about him asking for what he wants. I'm happy to give it; it just doesn't always occur to me to give it.

Ty: And it makes it so easy! Honestly, once I got over the need for pleasantries that we have in egalitarian relationships, it's great to be able to just say, "I want to cuddle, and this is the kind of cuddle that I want. Come pet my head." I can be really specific, and there's an ease to it that I don't find with people outside of the spectrum. It takes a lot of weight and pressure off of me, and takes a lot of complexity out of it.

Bella: "Normal" people seem to have a problem with people telling them, "I don't want to hug you, but I'm happy to shake your hand." They feel like there's something wrong. Or if you're asking a partner for something specific, like "I want you to touch my feet," they just get weird about it, and I don't really understand that part.

Ty: With her, there's consistently no judgment about the thing that I want and the way that I want it. She just takes it "as is". It's delightful. That same lack of judgment comes in when I make a correction. That "accepting correction with grace" thing? She does that exceptionally well, because she doesn't attach it to her ego.

Bella: If you're the ASD would-be slave in a potential M/s situation, I would advise making a list, as well as you can, about sensory issues, auditory issues, food problems, or anything else that might be a little strange or that someone might see as a potential problem. It might be a good idea to just write them all down, honestly, and just present that to your person. Being really up-front about that is going to make everybody's life easier, and our job as slaves is to give the master as much information as we can, so that they can make a good decision. So being able to look at yourself and write down all those weird things will help a lot. It would have helped quite a bit if I had had that knowledge when we first started.

Ty: From the top side of the slash ... well, I don't know if this is OK to say, but there's a part of me that wants to say that I hope this isn't your first rodeo, because you're going to need everything in your toolbox, and if you haven't sorted out your shit, it's going to be a challenge. A lot of the social graces which are assumed in most relationships aren't there. We have a dog who I would never recommend to be anyone's first dog, and likewise she's not someone I'd recommend to be someone's first sub. I know we all try to be open to everyone all the time, but that's not always workable.

As far as useful tools to help you, I would recommend learning something about Cognitive Behavioral Therapy. I'd also suggest having practical material that answers things in very simplistic ways to reference.

Bella: Doing bare-bones basic study about people on the autistic spectrum really helped to turn a lot of the struggles into common things which could be compensated for, or even turned into a positive thing.

Ty: Again, I'm really lucky that I work in an industry where I end up working with a lot of people on the spectrum, so over the years I've read a lot of books on how to work with or manage them. All of those have really helped me, so once we realized what was happening here, I could just apply all those learned skills.

Bella: One thing I'd like to say to the potential slaves is that for the right person, almost everything about your spectrum stuff is going to be useful somewhere. Yeah, you look at things differently than the rest of the world, and yeah, they say that it's abnormal when you do that, but it really can be very helpful in other spaces. Finding the places you can apply those different ways of thinking really successfully makes for a much sturdier slave.

Ty: If the person on the top side has their ego in check! People on the spectrum aren't necessarily going to blow sunshine up your ass. For fragile egos, that's hard. I've actually gotten to a place where I'm comfortable saying, "Hey, I need you to blow sunshine up my ass for the next five minutes."

Bella: It makes complete sense that we would be attracted to M/s in one way or another. This is an excellent way to have a life which has a stable structure and routine. I never have to wonder if I'm giving him what he needs, or if I'm acting rightly. It's really lovely. Honestly, it's the easiest relationship I've ever had in my entire life.

Interview with SaiTheBellaKitty

Some history: My Master Ki (Seikiji Heiwatori no Kiongakyu-Sensei) and I were together for a little over ten years, and they passed away last year from systemic scleroderma. We'd started out talking online and then we met in person at a party, and from there we built the relationship into a marriage and a full-time live-in TPE.

We had a lot more of a classic TPE dynamic in the beginning, but health challenges impact those things, and in the last couple of years we were in mostly a caregiver dynamic that was still service based. Even though they were severely ill and I was essentially doing hospice care, we still maintained protocols within the dynamic which kept both of us in the right headspace, feeling that we were as we should be.

They considered themselves an educator, a teacher, a trainer. They trained from the bottom up in a Japanese-feudal-style house; they had to earn their name and all of their privileges, similar to how you hear people describe Old Leather. Eventually they earned the title of Sensei, which meant they were proficient enough in their skills to teach them.

They were very big on using behavior modification and voice modulation to drop a submissive into the right headspace. They could use it to control a room, an audience, and myself.. They did not believe that being a Master or Owner meant that one was no longer in service; they considered themself to be in service to their community, and to our House. That meant they never got up on a high horse they were at risk of falling off of. They were very self-aware, willing to put in the work and learn everything about me.

I say all of that because I do have some interesting neurology—I have Dissociative Identity Disorder (DID) from childhood abuse, and I'm also diagnosed with ASD, although I was not diagnosed until my 40s. Once I was diagnosed, so many things made sense! I've developed many coping skills around my neurology, which is why I gave that history, as my Master was key in helping me put myself together.

Some parts of my autism were very positive for our dynamic. Being on the spectrum—for me personally—means that I do better when things are supposed to be done a specific way. I like it when there is a routine, an organized and understandable structure for how to behave, because then I know what I should or should not be doing. I don't have to ask myself, "How would a normal person react in this situation? I don't want to seem crazy." Our House has four "gates"— and the third one is to "always be appropriate"—those four rules helped me to answer that question for myself. It was an amazingly helpful tool.

My Master had studied psychology and was trained medically, so they were pretty sure even before I was diagnosed that I was on the spectrum, and because my Master had already figured that out, when we were building our own unique relationship structure together, they made space for those variances in my behavior. They designed the structure for my stability. For example, I do not adapt well to change; I can't turn on a dime. They could turn on a dime and decide, "Now we're going to do this or that," and I'd be stuck behind saying, "Wait! No, no, no!" If they said it was going to take two hours, I needed more warning if it was going to take four hours.

So we had a way for me to communicate, within the dynamic, that I was not handling a situational change well and that their decisions were causing me stress. Then they could take that into account, and we could go forward from there in a way that would help me cope with that better. It might be changing the order, or it might be just that they understood my struggle and would make accommodations for that, perhaps by giving me a chance to talk it out. "OK, you can vent for the next two minutes, but then you need to hush because this is what we are doing." They gave me space and understanding and acceptance.

I really think that acceptance of what's going on, and letting someone know that their feelings are heard, is one of the key components of dealing with a partner on the spectrum. If a person doesn't feel like they're being understood, they have an incredibly hard time trusting the other person. My Master's expression of understanding, and letting me know that my emotions were valid— perhaps irrational, but valid—helped me to get better control of them, and to behave more appropriately, both in the dynamic and in public spaces.

The ASD symptom which was the hardest to adapt to a power dynamic was this attitude toward change. On top of the ASD, I also have complex trauma from an unstable childhood, which made that worse. I felt that I needed control over what was happening on a day-to-day basis so that my brain wouldn't freak out. Giving up that control in a power exchange was initially very difficult, but accepting that my Master could provide that control for me in a healthy way was fantastic. However, that change issue was still hard for us up until the day they passed away.

I actually still struggle with it, at work, at home, wherever I am. I work on a pattern where I know what's going to happen, and a change, even if it's something positive, still makes me twitchy. Even if it's something I might really want to do, I don't want to do it. My brain wants a daily pattern so that I know what to expect and how to behave appropriately. When there's change, we have to figure out on the spot what masks we're supposed to wear, what behaviors we're supposed to do, and that throws me for a loop. Even if it should be obvious, my initial response can be an explosion.

We had rules about how I was to respond to changes. If my master said "Oh, by the way, we're doing things like this now," I was not allowed to freak out and scream, "No!" I could say, "OK, sir, what we originally planned was X, and this is a fairly large change, and I'm struggling with it." So I was expected to communicate that I was struggling, and *how much* I was struggling, and we would proceed from there. If it was not obvious, they would ask questions to clarify where my struggle was. Then we would break it down, and see if we could unknot it and stop it from being a struggle.

If it was obvious where my struggle was—if we'd been planning on having a quiet evening at home, and now we were going to run out and do three different errands—they would step in and say, "OK. We need to do these things, but this is how we'll handle it. We'll stop at McDonalds first and get you a hot fudge sundae." Or something similar, but it wasn't a bribe or a bargaining chip; it was a positive point added into what was, for me, a negative situation. During the ride, they would check in to see how I was doing. They might make accommodations for me: "You can stay in the van and listen to music while I go in here." After it was done, they would make sure to let me know that they were proud of me for getting through it.

I tried very hard to own my irrational responses, but I was not always capable of that. My job, though, was to look for the protocol. "OK, we know what to expect from the grocery store. Even though we didn't expect to be going there now, we have a protocol for dealing with the grocery store." It's like having a computer program—let's upload "grocery store" and then we'll know how to cope, and it will all be OK. I had to remember to keep telling myself that.

Being a slave, in general, was amazingly helpful for my ASD. After the first couple of years of getting everything on track, I knew how to phrase my communications. I knew they understood that I had irrational responses, but they accepted that part of me because they owned that part of me, just as they owned all of the good things about me. They were very clear that they owned every piece of me. "All of me" became a key phrase in our relationship, and it meant that they were aware and willing to take responsibility for the parts of me that were difficult or problematic, not just the fun and happy parts. We both would have loved to be able to hit a delete button and make those go away; that would have been fantastic, but that wasn't going to happen. Their acceptance meant that even if I wasn't always going to be able to meet our protocol standards—if I lost my shit—they would know that I had tried my best to control it, but just wasn't able to handle it that day. They didn't treat it as disrespect or failure, just as a glitch that was sometimes going to happen.

Once they felt I'd vented enough to mitigate my explosion, they would reel me back in. They might have me kneel before them, or pull me into a hug, or tell me to sit down and listen and let them speak. But I would be allowed that first minute of explosion, and knowing that I wasn't going to be punished or thrown away for something I couldn't help was huge.

This was not something I'd originally expected in an M/s dynamic, as slave or property. Once I got it, though, I realized that this was the real thing. This was not somebody who just wanted to own the good parts of me, or only own me when I was doing well. I could do that for a play partner, but for a 24/7 live-in dynamic, it really helped to know that I would always be accepted. Even if my irrational behavior triggered something in them, they would take the time to work on themselves and then they would come back to me and we could discuss it, resolve it, develop new coping skills. We could figure out what went wrong—was it a word? A phrase? A situation? Their willingness to work with me so that we could proceed in a positive direction showed me that even though I was property, we were still partners in the dynamic. My explosions were something to work on, to mitigate the next time it happened. Their control of the situation when I lost my own control meant that I could rely on them when it happened.

I'm actually very scared, now that they're gone, that I won't be able to do that on my own. I don't know if I'll ever find that again with someone else. I guess I will have to though, because even though they are not here, I still represent them, their training, and I represent myself. I may be scared, but I owe it to them to do my very best.

My master struggled with bipolar syndrome and childhood trauma. They were on medication and in therapy, and they had done a lot of work over the decades to gain control of it. But as we all know, sometimes triggers just happen, and sometimes I was the trigger. This was especially a problem if there was a time limitation—the change of schedule had come down, we had to leave in ten minutes, and they would not have the time or spoons to deal with me. They also had triggers around disrespect and rage. So if they got triggered by my response, they weren't always capable of calling a safe word, but I knew when a switch had been flipped. I also knew that it wasn't about me. They weren't angry at me, it was just internal anger which had been tripped. When that happened, it would immediately pause my personal meltdown. To explain that, I should talk about the "gates" (rules) in our House and relationship.

The First Gate is to take care of yourself. If you don't take care of yourself, you cannot take care of anything or anyone else.

The Second Gate is to take care of your responsibilities—to your pets, your children, your Master., etc. So if I saw that they needed me,

I would go straight to the Second Gate. It would trigger me to stop freaking out almost immediately, and help them. At the end of the day, I was theirs, and I was there to help them. I might just need to stop and give them a minute—sometimes they just needed some time to correct their headspace—or if it was worse than that, I knew what words to give them to help them come back down.

(Third Gate is to always be appropriate, and Fourth Gate is to keep your options open.)

Sometimes though, rationality just flies out the window. Our default, for these situations, was for one of us to use a safe word, because safe words are not just for scenes. They can be for conversations, or for life events. When I was unable to control myself and I could see that they were losing their ability to work with me—usually because I wasn't responding to what they were trying to do; I'd gotten too lost in my own meltdown to be able to respond properly, and even if they were saying, "Get on your knees", I wasn't doing it—that is when they would safeword on me.

They would say "Red!" and send me to my room to calm down. The safe word would stop the meltdown long enough for them to make sure that we would both be safe, and so they would be able to recover and handle me. That would last maybe five minutes, and then they would come check on me. It was not a punishment, it was a coping skill for us both. So safe words were what we used when everything was spiraling, and nothing we had set up was working.

Another problem was my sensory issues—textures, tastes, sounds, smells, that sort of thing. "I can't sleep on that because it's the wrong texture; I need to buy different sheets." I couldn't deal with the sound of kissing or the smell of chicken cooking. Especially early in the relationship, Master didn't understand why I needed physical things to be a certain way; this was largely because I didn't understand it either. I was irritated by everything but didn't know where it came from, so we had to work together to figure out why this was a problem. I'd learned in previous relationships that these complaints were not acceptable from an adult. My Master required that I poke at it, and find out where the actual problem was. They trained me to backtrack it and pinpoint the cause.

It was very frustrating for us both at first, because I did not have the communication tools, or the skill to dial it back until I found the problem. Their patience in teaching me this process made it safer, because we knew that the point was to find it and mitigate it. Certain chairs were problematic, as were certain sitting positions; stupid little things that would start me spiraling. (They actually made me remove "stupid" from my vocabulary, because these were legitimate triggers that needed to be respected.) If there were more than one trigger, they could build up and use up more of my spoons on each one. By the time I got to the fifth sensory issue, I would have no spoons and no control, and I would flip out for no apparent reason. If they noticed that I was not functioning properly, they would stop me and we would try to figure out where this had started. Some of the stimuli we could defuse, some we weren't ever able to eliminate and we just had to work through them. I just can't sleep on wrinkly sheets, so we had to buy sheets that weren't wrinkly so that we could accomplish this goal.

When we first got into this, I didn't think it would be possible for them or anyone to really master me, but their ability to understand and control their own self helped them to understand and control me. Their ability to maintain the control in the relationship, to inspire my submission and my desire to serve them every single day, even while they were actively dying, was because of that spark in them.

If I had to give advice to a dominant who is looking at a submissive with ASD: First, have the person with ASD write out a list of everything that bugs them, no matter how small. It can be a conversation if writing is a problem for them, or an open journal where they continually add to the document. Creating that list gives the dominant a starting place, and it gives the submissive a feeling of acceptance and validity. It means that the dominant understands that they have traits which are not normal, but are completely real and must be compensated for. The dominant needs to make it clear that they know there will be non-neurotypical responses, and they want to know all about them. It also gives the dominant an idea of if they are capable/compatible with this person and their particular challenges. There is no harm if that answer is no and the relationship discontinues. Better to know at the start than two years in.

Most people with ASD have a verbal or physical "stim response" when they are becoming stressed. If the submissive already knows what that is—"When I get anxious, my hands start flapping"—those should be shared. If they aren't aware of them, the left-hand-slash person needs to watch and observe the submissive, I sometimes hated the phrase, "Just observing," because that was what my Master did for the first year of our relationship.

They would get quiet in the middle of a conversation, and I would ask what was going on, and that's what they would say. "I'm observing". They were watching me to see whether my eyes or my forehead got tight, or my body language or way of speaking changed, or I started stuttering. They would look for these small paralinguistics and microexpressions to find the signals of something bothering me. This is super helpful for any dominant person to do, but especially so for a submissive with ASD. It gives you a huge amount of information on this person, and if you actually want to own a person, you need that level of understanding of them. How can you make decisions for them if you don't know how they work? How can you help them when they're going in a bad direction? You need to do a lot of observing.

I'd also suggest that to the submissives—pay attention to your Master and their expressions, and learn to consciously interpret them. If you know the signs that they're getting tired, you can be ready with a chair, or a useful suggestion. Learning this can be amazingly helpful, and since ASD people don't always come to this naturally, it needs to be a learned process. Once you've learned it for your Master, you realize it can also be helpful in the wider world as well.

A lot of these tools are helpful in any relationship - friends, family, work - but especially in a power dynamic and even more so in a dynamic with someone with ASD.

Sai (formal name Seikiji Heiwatori no Saishokyu-Shihan, a.k.a. Bella or The BellaKitty), brings 35+ years of Leather/BDSM experience and has topped, bottomed, served, mentored, trained, has had her girl collared for over 8 years, and was owned for 10+ years by her late Master Kiongakyu. She was mentored by Flagg of The Estate for 15 years and has studied and learned from many teachers over the years, including Jack McGeorge, Laura

Antoniou, and Raven Kaldera and his boy Joshua. She has also had contributions to books by Raven and Joshua, and Flagg.

She was trained from the bottom up and is experienced in multiple types of physical/emotional/psychological play styles, in addition to being well-versed in power exchange dynamics. She has been a board member of SMPEx and is active in a number of groups as both a member and a presenter. She enjoys sharing what she has learned during her journey and always hopes that her audience learns as much from her as she learns from them.

She can be contacted at via Fetlife as SaiTheBellaKitty.

Tools of Devotion: Perseverance in the Face of Challenge

Amanda Hamlin

My power exchange is a sacred duty for me. To be fair, I believe all committed relationships are a sacred duty and no one relationship style or dynamic is better or more holy than another. I believe it is part of that sacred duty to work towards creating the relationship structure, whatever it may be, that best serves the health and functionality of the relationship. That said, the degree of intentionality and deliberate structuring that are central to many power exchange relationships can bring this aspect into the forefront of consciousness much more strongly.

I have a tendency to see everything in life as a tool to a certain extent. I used to tell my students to view everything I taught them as a tool for them to store in their mental toolbox to be taken out and used later in whatever way worked best for them. Likewise, as someone committed to doing whatever it takes to nurture and protect my relationship, I want to make sure I have a well-stocked box of tools I can call on to help me do this. My concern is with the tool's effectiveness, rather than its nature, and I find power exchange to be a very powerful tool in this regard, which is why I am so invested in continuing to do it and building my abilities as a dom.

While each person is different, I think there are a few key reasons why power exchange can be especially beneficial to a relationship that involves neurodivergence. The very intentionality I mentioned is, in and of itself, extremely useful. Even if the relationship doesn't have a formal contract (we don't ... yet), there will almost certainly be lots of discussion about the specifics of the power exchange. The need for ongoing negotiations provides a safe space to discuss and address condition-related information and help guard against it being concealed or ignored. Since some tasks may prove difficult or impossible for a neurodivergent individual, having a clear division of labor and set of expectations can help relieve pressure in this area, as well as create a structure to help such an individual plan for and cope when having to tackle one of the "bad activities". Certain aspects of neurodiversity can make the presence of a leader role extremely beneficial in at least some areas of the relationship, and a power exchange framework can cast this necessity in a positive light, as well as putting important safety parameters in place. A good example would be how the executive function issues experienced by individuals with ASD and ADHD can make long-term, big picture thinking very challenging, and so having another member of the relationship take on the dominant role to hold the ultimate vision of the relationship and keep it on course for that vision may work well (though it can be exhausting for the person who has to make the big scary decisions without a lot of input from the ASD partner).

The best way I would describe our relationship structure would be as an ultra-casual 24/7 TPE, which sounds like a contradiction in terms. This means that I have the final word in all big decisions like money and medical care—and the rules for everyday life are always on, not just "in scene"—but they are on in the background. Most of the time we don't look like we are doing power exchange and mostly act like equals, but I can always bring the rules and structures back into the foreground any time I feel there is need or we are straying too far from them. Our dream relationship is a gender-flipped version of the traditional/vintage style (minus the 40s/50s décor) where he is my adoring homemaker and angel in the house who loves to nurture and pamper me and provides me with a secure refuge from the stresses of the world, and I am his protector and provider who interfaces with a harsh outside world that doesn't understand his condition so he doesn't have to. But that is fantasy, and we rapidly learned that our relationship diagnosis (see below) would render this impossible, at least in any sense other than than the extremely long term. For example, as a female-bodied individual I was trained in various homemaking tasks from an early age and didn't realize until we were deep in it that, as a male-bodied individual, he had received pretty much no such training, meaning I would have to supply it all from square one, a task rendered even more challenging due to the complications of his neurodivergence. So we do whatever we need to do to make things work on the practical level, and try to dress them up with the fantasy as much as we can, like getting him cute aprons to wear while cooking.

Things have rarely played out as expected, and being in a 24/7 TPE with a neurodivergent individual is very different than you would think based on the "standard" perception of such relationships. For one thing, my sub has never really expressed concern about what most people would consider the "big scary stuff" like having me totally control his money or his medical care. But he will fight tooth and nail over some minor change I want to make in his kitchen cleaning procedure, or even the suggestion that we do regular tasks in a different order just for today because we have other stuff going on, which was the exact opposite of the kinds of things I assumed would cause friction at the start of the relationship. Now it makes perfect sense to me, based on what I know about the ASD brain, the way it responds to structure (or lack thereof), the way it allocates focus to detail versus big picture thinking, and many other things. But I only have this baseline information because I have spent years researching the neurodivergent brain in an effort to make sense of seeming contradictions like the above. It does help. Now that I have the facts, when he resists something that, to me, seems incredibly minor for a reason that, to me, seems incredibly ridiculous and arbitrary, instead of blowing up in a combination of practical frustration and fear that that I'm a bad dominant ... sometimes, sometimes, on a good day, I am able to instead stop and ask "What ASD issue is this triggering for you?" It has been like learning a foreign language. It will probably never feel natural, but we have achieved a basic level of communication...most of the time. Even with all my research, he can still do things which completely baffle me.

Your Relationship Diagnosis

Trying to get a formal ASD diagnosis can be a real nightmare in and of itself, but it is important to remember that what we are dealing with here is not the simple fact of having a relationship that happens to contain one member who is neurodivergent. It has been said that neurodivergence tends to "come with friends and not the good kind" (Jessica McCabe in *How to ADHD*) and different conditions both within and between individuals can interact in ways that cause them to manifest very differently from the "standard" diagnostic presentation in isolation. Therefore, especially if you are a dominant who has to shoulder the burden of crafting a relationship structure that will best serve all its members, it is crucial to construct a relationship diagnosis that covers all conditions experienced by all members of the relationship, and the way those conditions impact each other. Unfortunately, no doctor is going to give you a relationship diagnosis. (It can sometimes be hard enough to get them to take into account interactions between conditions in a single individual. For example, I was never able to persuade medical professionals that my sub cannot take ADHD medication because it sends his ASD symptoms into nuclear overdrive.) The relationship diagnosis will have to come from careful observation, research, and trial and error that can take years and will be forever evolving as new data, both personal and scientific, is generated. This is, however, a crucial piece of information in the dominant partner's toolkit for crafting the best power exchange structure possible.

My relationship diagnosis is that my sub has ADHD and ASD while I have major depression and severe menstrual issues, both physical and emotional. Everything that follows comes through the filter of this relationship diagnosis. We do things the way we do because we have to in order to make them work given the unique constants we operate under. If something I say seems too extreme or not for you, remember: if your relationship diagnosis doesn't include all these specific conditions, you may not need it. On the other hand, if your diagnosis contains more or different conditions, that may make some of the strategies I propose unworkable for you. This is the problem with all "life hacks"—kink, vanilla, neurodivergent etc. All of them need to be modified to fit your unique circumstances. So do your research, get your relationship diagnosis, and then use it to filter everything I (and everyone else) says so it can be modified to work for your situation.

Another important part of the relationship diagnosis is figuring out what each member is looking for in terms of power exchange, what type of relationship structure they want or need, and identifying potential sites of friction or incompatibility. While this isn't the same as medical conditions, they do go together as conditions can impact what someone is looking for in this regard. I remember the first time I read Raven Kaldera's *Real Service* and identified my sub and I as being at opposite ends of the spectrum in terms of celebrity vs. parental dominance, which is almost certainly tied into our medical conditions. Because my depression makes me overwhelmed, unmotivated, and dissociated, my fantasy as a dominant is to be pampered and cared for, and to have certain aspects of life taken fully off my plate so I can focus my limited resources more effectively. However due to his ADHD and ASD, my sub needs (wants?) a high degree of oversight and micromanagement. He forgets things, gets overwhelmed, has trouble prioritizing, or needs to have the steps of a task spelled out in precise minutia. Our compromise, which really makes no one happy, is intense oversight during a training period, with the idea of trying to wean him off of it gradually so he can eventually do the task independently. I get overwhelmed frequently and don't keep up the level of oversight he requests, which sometimes frustrates him, and I also get overwhelmed and frustrated because his move towards independence is never as fast or complete as I hoped it would be. Wash, rinse, repeat. It's not ideal, but we are both stretching our conditions as far as we can to try to meet the other person in the middle and it works, only just, most of the time.

It is also crucial when dealing with any kind of condition or disability to make sure the relationship is a judgment-free zone with regard to those conditions. Certain aspects of certain conditions can render it impossible for the person who has them to meet certain needs another person has, needs that may also be condition-generated. It is an ongoing challenge to hold a headspace where one person is not portrayed as bad, attacked, or saddled with guilt for being incapable of meeting the other's needs, while simultaneously the other is also not bad or defective for having those needs, and the hurt and damage of those needs not getting met is not hidden or repressed. My depression-related neediness for physical and emotional comfort in times of high stress clashes directly with his ASD generated need to retreat into an isolated, predictable, and sensorially calm environment in those same situations. It is unavoidable that someone's needs aren't going to get met, someone is going to get hurt, and we have to find ways to live that reality without anyone suffering in silence or becoming resentful and lashing out. Ditto for our constant tug of war over his need for ever-greater structure and direction versus my need for more open-ended freedom and space to just *be*. But more on that later

Isolation and Overwhelm

I've seen articles claiming that the level of chronic stress experienced by single mothers of ASD children is so extreme that they can display symptoms analogous to soldiers serving in combat zones. This is not a test. This is not a drill. This is not a joke. While there certainly isn't an exact one-to-one correspondence between being a dominant and being a single mother, there is enough in common that those of us with ASD subs need to take this kind of claim extremely seriously. Although it is different from biological motherhood, in power exchange the reality of taking on responsibility for another human being can still be overwhelmingly engulfing. As someone who had never had nor wanted children, it was something I had never expected or intended to experience, and suddenly finding myself up to my neck in it felt unequivocally like drowning. I knew I was completely alone in the middle of the ocean. I could scream as loud as I wanted and no one would hear. My only options were to sink or swim, but now the one I loved most in the world was holding onto me, trusting me to also keep his head above water, even while making it harder for me to do so. If I let myself sink, he would sink with me, so the only option was to swim. The idea of power exchange went in a moment from being a fun, empowering game to being deadly serious.

Not everyone with an ASD sub will need to go it as alone as much as I do, but there are plenty of socio-cultural factors stacked against forming or maintaining strong support systems. Constant stress can change someone's personality, as can the burden of new responsibilities. In essence, I had to grow up very quickly with no warning, when I realized the limitations of his condition were much greater than either of us initially believed, and my friends were not so fond of the person I grew into. The fact that they also took the view that the empowered woman's solution to relationship problems was to leave did not help the situation at all. In general, socializing as a couple with your ASD partner can be challenging for reasons that are obvious to anyone who lives with someone with ASD. However, when you add power exchange into the mix, things can get even messier. Everyone has to make informed decisions about how out they want to be about their kink lifestyle, but the social challenges associated with ASD vis-á-vis internalizing behavioral systems can significantly reduce the amount of control you have over this decision. Integrating radically separate behavior codes for kink versus non-kink situations can be near impossible for a very socially challenged sub or, at least, training such a code may be an unrealistic use of your scarce resources. While my sub definitely knows not to call me master or use any of his submissive speech protocols in public, he still reads as submissive with absolute clarity. He speaks very softly, holds tight to my hand, often stands slightly behind me, and will usually defer to me, whether it's to answer questions about his life-course decisions or getting permission for what to order in a restaurant. Unfortunately, in the vanilla world, this sort of thing is likely to get me pegged as an emasculating bitch and cause him to be subjected to hectoring to "be a man". (I imagine there is a set of equally unflattering stereotypes for couples of other genders.)

The complications and potential stigmas surrounding the intersection of disability/neurodivergence and kink in the BDSM community itself that may inhibit its use as a form of social support have already been covered excellently by other authors so I will not do so again here; but there is also stigma, even indirect and unconscious, around power exchange in neurodivergent circles. As soon as my sub told me about his diagnosis, I started reading every book I could find about advice on being in a relationship with someone with ASD, and quickly discovered that such material often strongly emphasizes the necessity for the neurotypical partner to guard against the urge to become "controlling", to make absolutely sure they are not taking on a parental-type role, etc. If this is exactly what your ASD sub wants and needs, navigating through all this rhetoric can be hard, especially for a new dominant (or one who lacks confidence, like yours truly). If I had a dollar for all the times I've wrestled with anxiety over the possibility that I might be fooling myself about the whole power exchange thing and am actually just abusing and exploiting a disabled person, I'd be super rich by now.

An Overly Intimate Relationship with Protocol

Protocol never appealed to me. Even back when I first discovered the world of kink and was reading "general overview" books on the topic (back in the pre-internet days), I would always zone out or quickly page through the seemingly ubiquitous chapter on protocol topics like "slave training postures". It seemed incredibly futzy and boring in comparison with other aspects of kink. However, in my many attempts to research the topic, I've noticed a lot of discussion about that fact that people with ASD who are into BDSM tend to absolutely *love* protocol ... as in, they want protocols for everything, usually attributed to the comfort of knowing exactly what to expect in a given situation, or the expected response to a given stimulus.

While my sub has never expressed this sentiment directly, I have found that creating protocols for things is the most effective way to get him to regularly perform tasks to my specifications. So we have a lot of protocols—and no, they're not "sexy" protocols. We have protocols for cleaning the bathroom, for planning and then reporting on what he will/did buy while grocery shopping, for breaking down and disposing of the packaging that deliveries come in. Okay, being totally honest, a lot of these "protocols" are basically identical to the checklists and flowcharts that you can find in most vanilla literature for relationships, parenting, or self-help for individuals with ASD and/or ADHD. But dressing these systems up as protocols helps us feel better about them. This is a good example of Raven Kaldera's concept of power exchange as exoskeleton, as we are using our roles of dominance and submission as an overarching framework to reinforce and give positive context to something that could otherwise be highly unpleasant for us. Okay, I won't lie. It's still unpleasant most of the time. But integrating it into the power exchange helps keep in view that pushing through despite the unpleasantness is an act of commitment/devotion to the higher ideal of our relationship.

As I've said, these protocols are often very helpful in getting things done, but the other side of the coin is the danger of protocols taking over your life. It frequently feels like the need for more protocols or more detail and specificity for existing protocols is never-ending. If you also have ASD or just like extreme regularity and structure for whatever reason, this state of affairs may be great for you. However, most people like things to be a bit more open-ended and some, like me, have conditions where too much predictability and structure are actually detrimental to my mental health. In such cases, it is the dominant's job to set limits and make sure the protocols remain within humanly manageable bounds. Not having protocol at all can seem unbearable for the ASD individual, so often, the best strategy is to build flexibility into the protocol itself. Book-ending more free-form interactions with specific protocols that lead into and out of them can help serve as an anchor for the ASD individual.

In his book *ADHD After Dark*, Ari Tuckman describes the concept of "windows of willingness" which are designated times where all persons involved have agreed to be open to the possibility of a sexual encounter but the specifics of what will happen are left unspecified. Although the purpose in the book is to address sexual issues that may arise in relationships with neurodivergent partners, the applicability is much wider and can be used for virtually anything if you find yourself with a neurodivergent partner who wants to protocol everything under the sun to within an inch of its life. Whether it is a romantic evening, a kink scene, or working on home improvement projects, setting aside time but leaving the details up in the air can make sure it actually happens, and gives the ASD partner time to get in the right headspace while still allowing for some feeling of spontaneity in life. It is important to stress that using windows of willingness actually means going into the situation with no specific plan of what will happen, *not* having a plan in mind and just keeping it to yourself. Doing so could make the ASD partner feel deceived, unsafe, and reluctant to attempt this approach again.

However, I've also found that my sub himself seems extremely prone to making plans in his head and getting upset when they are disrupted because other individuals impacted by them didn't know they existed. This is one of the areas where I am constantly working on training him, both to be forthright enough to make sure everyone involved knows about essential plans, and to not get so attached and frustrated if a nonessential plan gets changed.

A final note regarding the ASD attachment to protocol: if deviation from pre-established protocol is absolutely necessary, the sooner the ASD individual can be made aware of the fact, the better. Frequently, just me officially declaring that I am suspending the protocol can be enough to calm him down and the really good news is that this can, with a lot of time and effort, become internalized. When disruptions happen in our normal daily flow, he is now sometimes able to just take a moment and mentally suspend protocol in his head, which enables him to be much less distressed by the disruption.

Communication Strategies I – Putting on the Brakes

Not being a sub myself, I used to imagine that "real" subs would (in the absence of extreme extenuating circumstances) always eagerly and enthusiastically obey. I've since learned, based on the accounts of many subs, that having a split second of resistance when given instructions is a normal human reaction. However, many subs train themselves to reduce this impulse or at least prevent it from showing externally, considering this to be an important part of the mental discipline of submission. Unfortunately, those with ASD and/or ADHD tend to have high emotional dysregulation and low frustration tolerance, which means this knee-jerk resistance reaction is likely to be much bigger than it would be for a neurotypical individual. Also, because people with these conditions can have a hard time regulating or even being aware of their external emotional presentation, said reaction is also likely to be a lot more obvious to the dominant.

Like me, you might find yourself asking, if subs with these conditions are really submissive, why do they respond so negatively when told to do something? Usually the answer has something to do with the command making the sub feel panicky or overwhelmed, but there can be more nuance to it. Common reasons I've encountered include: He was trying really hard to focus on something else and is frustrated about being interrupted. He was deeply hyper-focused on something and having to change gears too quickly was distressing. The task felt scary because it required more executive function than he felt capable of at that time, or it involved something new and/or a deviation from existing protocol, and the change from the expected or the lack of certainty was overwhelming. These are all valid experiences for neurodivergent subs. Usually when these issues come up, the subs aren't "bad" or trying to be difficult. However, this does not mean they have no impact on the dominant, especially when that dominant is under a lot of stress or grappling with depression, low self-esteem, etc, like me. In such circumstances, it can be very easy to have your already fragile sense of self-worth really shattered when your sub keeps blowing up or melting down every time you try to give instructions.

One possible solution is (you guessed it, more protocol) to require the sub to immediately do something by way of acknowledgment on receiving an order. This can help interrupt the knee-jerk resistance reaction and provide something else to focus on. It also forces a pause, to give the sub a chance to become aware of the reaction and put the brakes on. Our current protocol is for him to always respond to me with the phrase "As you command," to simultaneously induce him to pause and to give me positive reinforcement that being dominant is OK. Sometimes this may be all it takes. The sub may have been overreacting, and may realize after a moment's pause that whatever was provoking the resistance may not have been such a concern. However, there are times when the sub is in a state where the task will be impossible, or at least a poor use of resources (perhaps doing it will require dropping something more important), or the sub may feel that more information is needed to perform the task properly. (The amount of detail an ASD sub seems to want can reach near-insanity-inducing levels for the way my brain is wired.) It can even be something as simple as "Give me five minutes to finish what I'm doing now so I don't have to switch gears mid-task." Unfortunately, especially when the sub is already in a state of heightened emotion, this information can easily be conveyed in a way that reads as angry or defiant. So we are constantly working on an ever-evolving set of submissive speech protocols to enable him to give and get the information he needs without inadvertently coming across as resistant.

Another thing which is frequently mentioned regarding the neurodivergent is the concept of face blindness, usually associated with their inability to read the non-verbal cues of others. Based on my experience, I've become convinced that this may also lead to a lack of awareness of one's own non-verbal cues. I've had way too many situations involving interacting with someone with ASD who repeatedly denies being angry while displaying voice tone, facial expression, and body posture that read to me as anger. Even if the other person is truly sincere about not wanting to project anger; even if, intellectually, I know this fact; my nervous system still interprets the non-verbal cues as anger and goes into alert mode, increasing the difficulty of calm, rational communication. For this reason, we have decided that all serious, stressful relationship communications and negotiations should be conducted, as much as possible, through a computer messaging system rather than verbally in order to eliminate any unintended non-verbal stresses. This also has the added benefit of relieving some of his anxiety around verbalization, as it gives him more space to plan out what to say, as well as the ability to look back over the conversation and keep the different aspects of it fresh in his head.

I will sometimes demand one of these online discussions if an emergency comes up or if I feel the conversation we're having is becoming too heated, but the majority are scheduled. We have multiple check-in discussions each week to bring up issues that need addressing, talk about what is or isn't work with the strategies we implemented in the last meeting, or propose and negotiate new rules. This has turned out to be crucial, because he has a hard time getting in a headspace to be able to problem-solve or use the kind of big-picture higher-executive-function these kinds of tasks require. He would get panicky when put on the spot in this regard, and not be able to come up with anything. This was particularly frustrating to me, because he was also constantly shooting down all of my ideas—something I've now realized is directly related to the ASD resistance to change and fear of not knowing what to expect. I frequently now take the approach that if he can't think of a better idea, we're just going to do it my way for a few weeks, with the option that he can renegotiate after that point if it turns out to be unbearable to him. In the vast majority of cases, this is sufficient time to allow him to get over his ASD discomfort with the unfamiliar. By the time the end of the test period rolls around, if he even remembers it at all, he has now succeeded in acclimating to the new thing and it usually turns out to need little or no modification. Of course, this is frequently accompanied by the need to implement changes gently and gradually (or what I refer to as an enraging slowness that makes snails look fast). For example, new rules need to be implanted in three stages, each several weeks long: an acclimation period where he gets used to the rule, a training period where I need to aggressively remind him every time the rule is not properly implemented, and finally, an integration period where he will actually receive a penalty for not applying the rule correctly.

Rules can be tricky in other ways as well. The ASD tendency towards habit means that rules that don't come up for a while can cease to be part of his mental landscape. Or if he is supposed to ask permission for something, if a long time passes without me denying permission, he gets accustomed to that and starts feeling entitled to it. Then, when a situation comes up where enforcement is necessary, I get hurt and frustrated that the rules went "offline," especially because his desire to have so many specific rules means that enforcing all of them all the time would be too much for either of us, and he feels betrayed because he feels like I am being unfair and "changing things" on him.

The accusation that I am changing things or "goal-post-shifting" is perhaps one of the most ubiquitous aspects of our interactions. It can really make me want to yank my hair out, especially when I feel strongly that no change has occurred and he has simply forgotten or misunderstood the rule, but I understand that, on some level, it strikes at the very core his ASD need for routine and clear expectations. He also has an extreme paranoia about being treated unfairly, probably because of having many people when he was younger not understand and/or not care about the limitations of his condition. The only solution I've found is to keep a log of all the rules (or as much as is humanly possible—both the number and complexity of the rules he requires would make a complete log very unwieldy). This doesn't stop the rules from going offline or from both of us getting hurt when they do, but he seems to recover emotionally more quickly when I can point to the rule in the log, and he sees that I wasn't actually being arbitrary or breaking protocol.

Another issue where his ASD communication issues come up is the fact that he is very much what is referred to in the kink community as a brat. He loves to needle me, to pretend to resist or not do things right, and gets a thrill out of having me get irritated. I don't handle bratting well. Because of my insecurities, this behavior often feeds that voice of doubt in my head telling me I'm a bad dominant or that he secretly doesn't actually want this in the first place. Because of the high level of stress that often accompanies living with and caring for a neurodivergent individual, I can lose patience pretty quickly, go into frustration overload, and lash out.

This becomes a big issue in two ways. First, because of his inability to read non-verbal cues, he can have a really hard time picking up on the fact that my stress level is maxing out and, if that does happen and I do get angry, his emotional dysregulation makes him likely to be hurt, overwhelmed, or have a meltdown. Our solution to this is that I have a "top safe word" that I can say to let him know when I feel like I'm approaching a threshold in terms of stress or frustration and heading for overwhelm; and because it is simple and straightforward, he is much more likely to pick up on it than on non-verbal cues or even more complex verbal explanations. Like most things here, it's still a work in progress, but it is another tool we are trying to train ourselves to use. Even a joking reference to the fact that he has about used up his "brat fuse" may be effective and he will also, sometimes, be proactive and ask me how big the "brat fuse" currently is.

Communication Strategies II – Navigating Dynamic Situations

The inability to pick up on non-verbal cues and make executive decisions based on them can have much more serious impacts than him simply not knowing when to stop bratting. My depression is in flux constantly and the type of service and support I need from him can change a lot based on how bad it is. He has developed the habit of regularly asking me to rate my depression on a scale of 1 to 10. This is simple enough that I can do it even when I am very depressed, and he has certain categories of behavior associated with the different levels that he knows to bring into play depending on my answer. While the margin of error is decently large, the communication difficulties we face make it a lot better than nothing.

On a somewhat related note, if the relationship contains any female-bodied individuals, it is important to keep in mind the possible interplay between the menstrual cycle and neurodivergence. Certainly there can be a lot of potentially disruptive interactions between hormonal cycles and symptoms of neurodivergence in the same individual which could require modifications to normal systems and protocols and more research on these interactions is emerging all the time. My personal experience, however, is about when the person with neurodivergence does not personally menstruate, but is still significantly impacted by the menstrual cycle of other people in the relationship. Similar to (and frequently overlapping with) depression, menstruation involves shifting needs and adaptation to new situations. For us it is usually a time when he has to take on extra duties while simultaneously receiving less direction and oversight from me, which is not a fun combination for a sub with ASD. However, unlike depression, menstrual cycles are usually at least somewhat predictable, so the dominant in such situations should either assign someone to monitor cycles or personally take on that duty. The person with ASD needs as much of a heads-up as possible to prepare for the shifts.

This leads to the final point in this section: the need for an emergency plan. Jawn's interview in *Mastering Mind* talks about the need for dominants with depression to institute "standing orders"—orders that are always "on"—and the sub knows are to be obeyed even when the dominant isn't in a position to enforce them, thereby ensuring that the dominant will receive proper care when incapacitated by depression. Because of my combination of depression and menstrual issues, I have to be "offline" a decent amount of the time, so I know that making a good emergency plan is crucial for me, but I think it is something all dominants could benefit from. Even if you don't have conditions that regularly incapacitate you, anyone can get sick or have a crisis at work, resulting in less time and energy that can be devoted to actively being in charge. In any relationship, having at least the skeleton of an emergency plan can be seen as a courtesy to the sub, as it will make the job easier even for a sub who is relatively comfortable acting independently. If the sub has ASD, such a plan is not a courtesy. It is a definite necessity—that oversight, structure, and clear expectations thing again. Of course, without direct oversight, even with a solid emergency plan, the ASD sub will probably not be able to do as much as they would normally, so the emergency plan should focus on what is most absolutely necessary. Ours involves keeping my immediate surroundings neat (mess stresses me and can amplify my depression), maintaining basic hygiene standards in key areas (like the kitchen), making sure everyone eats reasonably healthy food, and checking up on me to make sure I don't skip essential self-care tasks like hydration and exercise.

Also, emergency plans are not just for doms. Subs can become incapacitated too. My sub can experience emotional meltdowns or sensory processing overloads related to his ASD that can put him out of commission for a few hours up to several days. For example, it is a given that he will not be good for anything for about a week around the Fourth of July each year, due to the over-stimulation caused by all the people setting off fireworks close to our house. During times like this, we need a plan in place for how to get the essential things on the emergency list done, but this time with his reduced input. The most challenging aspect of this usually involves food. The kitchen is his domain (meaning that he mostly gets to do what he wants with it), but the state of (dis)organization of the refrigerator and cabinets, while it may make sense to his neurodivergent mind, makes even simple acts like making a cup of tea or a pb&j sandwich difficult for me. We don't have a good solution to this yet but are constantly tweaking our approach. I have a dream of filling everything in the kitchen with those stackable drawers, but that is a very long-term project. Due to our complex relationship diagnosis, the times when both of us are at full capacity are usually in the minority, and having a solid emergency plan allows us to keep things mostly functioning when one or the other of us goes offline. (Then there are the times when we both get incapacitated at the same time and there is really no solution to that.)

Honoring Limits

Over the years, I've read far too much BDSM literature that seems to take a rather negative view of limits—like having less limits is a positive thing (outside the requisite "no children, animals, or dead people") or that working to overcome limits is somehow self-edifying and an important part of one's emotional/spiritual "growth". The part that I find most frustrating about this attitude is that the actual impact of the limits seems not to matter—whether or not they are causing concrete difficulties for an actual person in the real world. Rather, it seems that the mere fact a limit exists means that challenging it is good. I've always taken the "if it isn't broke don't fix it" attitude to limits, both kink and otherwise. I have a massive fear of heights and falling sensations. Because of this I've never been on a roller coaster and have no intentions of ever doing so, as I can think of no realistic situation where I would *need* to be on a roller coaster or derive any benefit from being on one. However, the same fear can be a significant barrier to air travel and, when I was offered a much-needed job which required overseas travel, I put absolutely everything I had into finding a way to make doing so possible.

I mention all this because the neurodivergent sub is likely to have all kinds of strange limits relating to many aspects of life; which the sub perceives to be, and some of which may in fact be, completely rigid and non-negotiable because they relate to the sub's neurological wiring, which not even they have control over. Taking the approach that limits are there to be challenged is likely to cause a lot of grief for you and/or the sub in this kind of situation. You need to be prepared to at least be open to respecting and not messing with these limits, no matter how quirky, arbitrary, or inconvenient they are. On the other hand, it is also important to keep in mind that dominants also have limits. You have to, first, be honest with yourself when you hit a limit, and also be very clear with your sub about situations where the needs of the sub's condition are hitting a hard limit for you, and that you simply cannot accommodate in this situation. This is not something to be taken lightly—as it can be very costly to the sub—but the dominant also needs to sustain a high level of functionality to properly manage the relationship, so you must do what you must to stay at that level.

Because of sensory processing issues and emotional issues related to his condition, my sub has a massive range of things that are upsetting to him if they are not said or done in particular ways. Wanting to be a nice person and non-ableist, I tried to accommodate all of these needs. Unfortunately, I did not realize at the beginning of the relationship that having so many tiny things I had to keep track of, which required me to be always overlooking and monitoring my own behavior, was making my own dissociation worse and creating a damaging state of hyper-vigilance. About four years into the relationship, he had to stay overnight at a medical facility for a sleep study and we were apart for the first time since he moved in. I was overwhelmed by the sense of liberation I felt just from drinking a glass of milk and realizing I didn't need to be constantly trying to control how I drank it in order to not make noises that would overstimulate him. That was when I understood we had a big problem, and I would need to correct things for the sake of my own sanity. While I still take his accommodations very seriously, I also have times when I have to draw a line and say, this is too much, too restrictive. This is a hard limit because it will impair my ability to do my job as the dom.

And yes, I feel super guilty about this. Yes, I feel selfish and insensitive about putting my needs first. Yes, I feel weak for having limits. I would be the last person to shame anyone for feeling this way. Feel however you feel as long as you do right by your sub. Every community and subculture comes with a set of ideals about what relationships should look like. This ambivalence about limits is just one example in the kink sub-culture. There are many more and, if your identity also involves feminism, the queer community, Neo-Paganism, or a broad list of other possibilities, they also have their own ideals that may or may not be compatible with each other, or with power exchange. This is an issue that everyone has to deal with, but having a neurodivergent sub pretty much guarantees that your relationship will diverge wildly, at least in some ways, from the models.

I'm not going to tell you that you have to be okay with this, that you have to find a way to stop believing the voice that whispers that you're really a failure as a dominant. Why can't you get your sub to do this or that, the way all the other doms can? I have depression and I have that voice yelling at me almost continuously. I have not silenced the voice, I have not gotten over it or convinced myself it's false. It is still there all the time and it still hurts. What you absolutely need to do, is find a way to not let any doubt or shame you might feel about the need to modify your relationship from the kink ideal impact your decision making. Yes, I cry and feel like crap about it a lot, but when the chips are down, I find a way to do what I have to do despite it. Your sub is counting on you, which is true for every dominant, but a sub with ASD is likely to especially crave the stability and security of being able to trust the dom to guide the relationship, and, due to issues with unfamiliar situations and executive function, to be less able to step in and help if you fall apart.

Not everything related to ASD and limits is super grim-dark and serious like I portrayed here. By way of a more light example, his sensory processing issues mean he cannot stand to have anything touch his neck. As we both find various neck-related erotic activities appealing, this is a bit disappointing but, above and beyond that, this essentially prevents him from wearing a collar. Because it negatively impacts both of us, although in a small way, this is a limit we've made a commitment to challenging and trying to work through, primarily through very gentle, gradual exposure. It's not a high priority. We don't *need* a collar to make us feel our relationship is real, but it is something we do care about. Actually, since I started writing this I got him his first "practice collar". It's a cheap fuzzy fashion choker for teen girls, nothing to write home about. But the idea was to get something that was softer and more flexible than a traditional collar as well as less of an investment in case it turned out to be a complete no-go. He definitely is nowhere near being able to wear it on anything remotely approaching a permanent basis, but he can keep it on for more than a few seconds without freaking out and we think that's good. The point is, I'm not saying you should never challenge any limits. Just pick your battles and only challenge a limit when you have a good reason to—meaning there is a clear concrete benefit that outweighs the stress of trying to work through the limit; knowing that when dealing neurodivergence is involved, said stress is likely to be pretty high.

Scarce Resources

In the modern world, there never seems to be enough time, money, or energy, no matter who you are, but the need to carefully allocate scarce resources goes up to eleven when dealing with neurodivergence. Things which seem simple and straightforward almost never are, and often end up requiring far more from one (or more) of the above limited budgets than might have been guessed going in. One of the most challenging jobs I have encountered as a dominant is how to determine priorities and allocate resources in the most effective way possible when there is never enough to go around. Right now I have to decide whether I should I allocate my time and energy to finding a doctor for myself, doing a better job monitoring his exercise to protect his health, trying to find more paid employment, repairing the sink and/or refrigerator to avoid expensive repairs later, or to taking it easy in the hopes of staving off that next round of burnout I'm teetering on the edge of? I can only do one, maybe two if I'm really lucky, and the strain of making the decision is, in and of itself, draining. There is no one right answer to this, as the needs in each relationship will vary based on the relationship diagnosis.

I tend to rely a lot on "robot slaves," as I call them, to lighten the workload, those wonders of modern technology designed to automate almost anything. However, as with anything, there is a trade-off. Not only do robot slaves come with a high up-front cost, learning new technology will take time and effort and can be frustratingly buggy, especially for an individual with ASD who has difficulty adjusting to new ways of doing things.

Also, resorting to technology will not solve all the problems for the ASD partner. Although we have a robot vacuum that can be programmed to run on a schedule, because the noise it makes still causes sensory issues for my sub, finding times when we can actually set it to run are challenging. Ultimately, it is necessary to weigh the costs of dealing with technology against the costs of having a human do the same task. I've been told that the time I have to spend doing periodic maintenance on the robots as well as making sure they get fixed if they malfunction is actually greater than if I just did all the work myself. This may or may not be true, but it is a different kind of time. Doing maintenance on technology tends to require large chunks of time occasionally, while doing things manually involves doing lots of little jobs through the day. Since motivation and initiation are a challenge for me—a trait which I share with my ASD sub and, based on my research, lots of people with ASD and ADHD—it makes sense to find ways to consolidate jobs into large chunks. We both work better under these conditions, whether through the use of technology or just restructuring how a job is done, such as planning out blocks of meals in advance.

Of course, this is not always possible. One of my sub's most hated jobs is the tidying-up checklist he has to complete every day, because it is just that—lots and lots of little tasks. We have attempted to streamline things by having the list on an app so that it auto-renews every day, and we can both access it from our phones so that I can easily check up on him and make corrections to the list that show up in real time. Also, the app is necessary for my sanity because the list is massive. One of the ASD accommodations he needs is for every single step of each task to be a discrete item on the checklist, and many of those items need to be very detailed and worded in a specific way. Dealing with all of this in paper format was unmanageable for me. However, even though technology makes the book-keeping and maintenance on the list much easier, there is no way around the fact that he has to actually physically go do every single item on it each day, and we are still struggling with figuring out how to make this practically effective and emotionally tolerable.

In general, although I have the prerogative to assign him jobs, he has the right to require me to accommodate his condition with regards to those jobs, whether that is buying something to make doing it easier, modifying the environment, or designing a new system to facilitate the job. Finding the correct combination is an ongoing process with a lot of trial and error, which is one of the reasons costs tend to be so high. For example, he has negative sensory reactions to both abrasive surfaces and strong-smelling chemicals, so we have tried many different approaches to find effective cleaning methods that use neither and are still looking. It is important to keep in mind too that, great as technology is, sometimes exactly the opposite is called for. We actually got rid of our power mower and got a push mower because the noise of the power mower was overstimulating him. For the same reason, even though I think vacuuming is more efficient, I usually grant his request to be allowed to sweep instead of vacuum when spot-cleaning small areas, because for us the greater time and energy that it takes for him to do these tasks manually are outweighed by the high cost (on every front) if he was to become overstimulated. Everything is a balancing act and an exercise in priorities.

Refilling the Tank: Self Care and Fun Together

Given that resources are so limited, getting burned out is an ever present-risk. Again, this is a concern for everyone, but the risk definitely goes up when neurodivergence is involved. Knowing the best way to put gas back in your tank so you can keep dealing with all the stresses is crucial. Everyone's self-care needs will be different, so taking some time to figure out what helps you recharge is important. I personally really enjoy quality tea, chocolate, and hard cider, as well as scented candles, perfume oils, and even unusually-flavored lip balms. The reason these things are so beneficial for me is because of my tendency to dissociate. The stress related to working around his ASD makes being present in my body even more difficult, so having things that I can turn to as a mini-sensory-indulgence helps me ground back into the physical, which in turn greatly improves my emotional regulation. The fact that I have developed a regular yoga practice and an epic skin care routine are also related to my efforts to feel physically embodied. While I may dream about luxury vacations, gourmet multi-course meals, or day long spa treatments, the above things have the benefit that most of them don't require a lot of effort and can be fitted in even when we are in a time crunch and overwhelmed. Even in the most stressful times, I can still light a candle, take a ten-minute break to do face yoga, pause to savor my morning tea, or just breathe in the smell as I put on lip balm. Struggling to be present in your body may not be your Achilles' heel, but whatever that is for you, it is important to find it and find ways to address it, some of which you can draw on even when both of you are offline.

I also like to make myself a hot water bottle and have a lot of comforters, throws, and shawls on the couch so I can make nests out of them and snuggle up with my cats. Among other things, this kind of cuddling and cocooning helps me deal with touch deprivation, a common concern for those whose partners have ASD. While it would be untrue to say he never desires physical contact, he frequently will have no active interest or even be averse to it, often enough to clash with the level of such contact I need. Of course, I could order him to do it, but while he would willingly go through the motions, I would still be able to detect his emotional state, which is beyond his control and which would make the situation agitating, rather than relaxing for me. It would also prevent him from taking care of himself and getting into a better headspace where he would be more able to care for me later. So I mostly try to take care of myself in these situations, and lots of blankets and cats help fill the gap.

This last raises the point that subs also need self-care, and for individuals with ASD, this will probably look like having a private, secure, sensorially neutral space to retreat to if things get too overwhelming. Using electronic devices can be soothing as they are controllable and predictable, and a weighted blanket and/or seating that allows one to bounce or rock can provide comfort. So he has his rocking chair in front of the computer and it is very much his space. He got very upset one time when I tidied it up, thinking I was doing him a favor. It may be frustrating to dominants to have something about which they have to be so hands-off, but the sense of stability and control is so crucial to individuals with ASD. Those who have nuerodivergent subs should strive to give them their own room, or at least have their special space be behind a curtain or screen or inside a closet or cabinet that can be closed up when not in use. This is both to promote an "out of sight, out of mind" mentality and prevent potential eye-sores to avoid triggering the dominant's urge to mess with it, and to reassure the sub that the space is secure and safely sealed away from the rest of the world.

It is worth noting that individuals with ASD and/or ADHD can be somewhat prone to addictive behavior. Scores of accounts have been written by parents of such children about their ability, if left to themselves, to spend days at a time on their electronic devices without seeming to notice. Individuals with these conditions may also be prone to eat and drink to excess. Going cold turkey on all of this is probably not recommended (that thing about people with ASD hating changes), but it will probably be the dominant's painful duty to exert some kind of restraining influence. This can be very painful if you are like me and also enjoy video games and good food and drink. For my sanity as well as his, there have to be times when indulgence is OK, but it is my job to enforce limits (and model good behavior even when I really don't want to). All the alcohol and chocolate in the house is hidden away in a place only I have access to, he has to ask permission to eat certain foods (like desserts or frozen pizzas), and he is not allowed to pester me about ordering take-out from restaurants.

His computer is also hooked up to a device so it will only turn on for a set amount of time when he inserts a token. He gets a controlled amount of these tokens, so he can choose to use them as needed to retreat while there are still clear limits, without me getting dragged into too much micromanagement. This token system is a good example of how any relationship system is a work in progress. Many years ago we tried having only designated computer times, enforced with parental control software, then padlocking the computer cabinet and requiring him to ask for the key. When we did get the token box, we started with me having to provide tokens each day, then each week, and we've finally moved to two weeks (an example of the concept discussed in the last section about how, whenever possible, daily small jobs should be converted into occasional big jobs). The point is that there should be no pressure about getting a relationship system right on the first try. It can take years of playing with one system after another to find one that clicks with your relationship diagnosis.

Keep in mind as well that your sub can be a useful tool in your self-care system, but also that neurodivergence can come with unexpected challenges and restrictions in this area. For most of my life, if someone had asked my what I found most appealing about the idea of having a sub, I probably would have said "Free massages whenever I want." Sadly, my sub has dysgraphia and fine motor impairments, not uncommon for individuals with ASD, so free massages are simply not on the menu at all. I have provided tools and trained him in techniques related to cupping and wood therapy so he can still provide soft tissue manipulation without using his hands, but even this frequently does not fit into the necessary allocation of scarce resources. However, fairly simple tasks—like making a hot water bottle or serving tea—he has been able to integrate into his routine with relative ease. He also screens my calls (which he does not like) and selectively blocks my internet browser to protect me from distracting or depressing material when I'm trying to recharge, and on top of everything else, he's an amazing cook. He has mastered the ultimate cooking benchmark, as presented in *Real Service*, of "being able to make comfort food just like the dom's mother/grandmother" and we are both incredibly proud of this fact.

Finally, an important part of refilling the tank is spending quality time together. Dealing with things like neurodivergence can become so all-consuming that, power exchange or no, the relationship itself can wind up taking a back seat. The dominant needs to be on the watch for this and institute procedures to keep it from happening for the well-being of all involved. We have a night every week for playing video games (which is super meaningful because it is how we met), as well as a night for watching movies/TV. The latter is my gift to him as it isn't something I particularly enjoy, with the understanding that I have to approve his viewing selections and he isn't allowed to ask me to watch things at other times (this used to be a big problem). We also have a romantic date night every month, and continue to look for more ways to build spending time together into our routine.

Closing Thoughts

All of the above is just personal narrative and suggestion. When it comes to relationships, there are no rules, there is no "normal." He and I lived on opposite sides of the globe and met online via our youtube channels. He was only a year into college and had never left home, held a job, or had a romantic relationship, much less done anything related to power exchange. Although I was older and had an employment history, my experience with relationships in general and power exchange in particular was still what most would consider pretty minimal. Because of the distance and cost involved, visits weren't really an option. The day we met for the first time in person is the day he moved in with me, and also the day we, at least nominally, started our 24/7 TPE, with no negotiations, no contract, nothing. In short, according to conventional wisdom, we did everything "wrong". But almost ten years later, we are still here, and if not more in love than we ever were, at least more than we were for many years. Yes, there has been, and still is, a lot of pain and suffering. We've had to go back and painstakingly build systems where we started thinking we could just fly by the seat of our pants. The writing of this document has been interrupted innumerable times by various practical and emotional crisis that required immediate attention while working on it, in addition to the fact that every time we had a fight or relationship issue—especially if it involved me failing to properly apply one of the principles set out here—I would decide I wasn't going to submit this essay after all, since I clearly had no idea what I was doing and couldn't possibly claim to be an authority on the subject.

There are ways we are and always will be a very bad match, like the differing environmental and emotional needs of depression vs ASD, like celebrity versus parental dominance. But there are also other ways in which we are clearly meant for each other. This, for me, is the heart of committed relationship as sacred duty—not pretending the relationship or the other person is perfect or even that you are okay with them not being perfect, but still putting your all into working with what you have. He is not an easy person to live with. Neither am I. It takes both of our rock-solid dedication and every tool we can get our hands on to keep things running.

I always say that the little tiny things are what are most important in a relationship. For me that would include the fact that he got me a mug with imagery from one of my favorite (obscure) video games on it, and always says "Be careful, warrior," a line from the game, when he serves me tea in it. It includes how he plates my food to look like an angry face when I'm having a bad day to show sympathy, the way he laughs with total abandon when we watch comedy shows— things that are totally, achingly sweet and make me feel seen and understood and connected the way nothing else ever has.

But most of all, we feel safe together. We both have conditions that require us to take things slower than mainstream society says is OK. We both need a degree of patience, tolerance, and accommodation that is not readily forthcoming in the "normal" world but which, in the relationship, we know is in the other person's best interest to provide. After all, they need it too, and we both know the shoe could be on the other foot the following day—or in the next five minutes.

Remember that anything can be a tool. The relationship is what is important, not what tools you use to maintain it. It is my hope that this document has provided you with a few more tools to stash in your mental toolbox, to be saved, modified, and pulled out as needed, to enhance your own relationship, regardless of your specific relationship dynamic or diagnosis.

Amanda is an aspiring fantasy novelist with a lifelong interest in the Middle Ages and alternative spirituality. She and her sub met in 2013 via their online gaming channels and he traveled all the way from the Land Down Under to be with her. When not wrestling with the practical aspects of life, they spend their time happily playing video games, Dungeons and Dragons, and working on various creative projects together.

ASD, PDA, and M/s

Hello! I'm Ashtyn and I'm autistic with a pathological demand avoidance (PDA) profile and a slave in a Master/slave (M/s) dynamic! While it seems like a specific set of internal processes and external behaviors, it is different for everyone who experiences it. My own brand of autism could be the same in name as yours but look different inside and out. We are people, after all, not profiles.

First off, let's define a demand. A demand can be social rules, promises, expectations, pecking order, or many other things. Basically, demand avoidance involves not being able to do things for yourself or others at certain times. We all do this to some extent, but marked demand avoidance is a significant trait in the PDA profile.

So what exactly does this look like for me?

- ❖ High levels of anxiety in social situations.
- ❖ Strong need for control over environment and routines.
- ❖ Underlying difficulty in understanding social interactions.
- ❖ A required level of sameness and rigidity in routines.
- ❖ Intense focus, often on other people, to the point of obsession.
- ❖ Resistance to and avoidance of demands (even if familiar with the activity/task).
- ❖ Difficulty following instructions or complying with rules.
- ❖ Need for autonomy and agency within relationships.

Ostensibly, this list is almost entirely in conflict with a M/s dynamic. As a slave, I give up control. I must follow instructions and comply with his rules. I give up my rights to autonomy and agency. I navigate social interactions for him. It seems fundamentally opposed to the M/s handbook to have a brain that works this way. However, my Master and I have learned ways to cope and thrive.

Our relationship takes a collaborative approach with negotiated demands and expectations. Unilateral decision making doesn't happen often without conversation. I need to feel like my thoughts and feelings are heard even if I don't get the final say. We keep the lines of communication completely open at all times. This requires a lot of emotional regulation on both our parts. Neither one of us wants to fly off the handle and call the other an "asshole," right?

Master is patient with me when giving instructions. He sometimes has to repeat himself or text me instructions instead. He makes things easier to do. For example, brushing my teeth is one of the hardest demands in the book! He often brushes his teeth with me to help settle the avoidant knee-jerk. However, this doesn't always work. We're realistic about what I can accomplish in a given day.

As for being resistant to demands, it's impossible to completely erase. I have to be very open with Master about my ability to do things. I can literally just say "I can't do that right now" and we can discuss further. Obedience isn't the foundation of our relationship, it's understanding.

We've also decided on the term power slave for me. It means I function with a high level of autonomy within the M/s framework following his guidance. Basically, he tells me where he wants to go, and I figure out how to get there. This closely ties in with anticipatory service insomuch as I anticipate the paths he would want. I don't always choose the right one, but every mistake is a learning opportunity.

The M/s framework for protocols and rituals mimic my need for sameness in routines. For example, from a very early age I needed to always walk on the same side of people. My friends were baffled but complied. Now, walking to the right and behind is a protocol in which I revel. Additionally, we have a morning ritual which I follow with rigidity. It feeds the part of me that needs sameness to function.

The pathological demand avoidant profile for an autistic can mean one needs a high level of autonomy in life. A PDA profile does not mean one cannot be a slave. With trust, empathy, and communication, anything is possible. Using the M/s framework might even be helpful for someone with this profile by providing structure in routines.

Interview with the Goddess Indigo and Dr. Bob Rubel

The Goddess Indigo: We first met when my boy was brand new. He'd ended up at a kink party at an Arabian horse farm, where I was teaching a class. He actually hit it off with my partner, who also had a PhD, and he seemed to think that I was OK because I was partnered with another PhD. He told us that he had come in from the swinging community, and he didn't quite seem to understand what it was that we were doing. But he thought it was really cool, and he wanted to take pictures of us. That's how new he was—he wasn't even thinking about it for himself yet. He thought I was exotic-looking, and would I be OK with him taking pictures of me? And my answer was No. He was very charming, but the idea of someone taking pictures of what it is that we do who didn't even understand or appreciate it wasn't going to work for me.

Dr. Bob Rubel: I just wanted pictures of you! I didn't need to see you playing, I just wanted to be able to look at you again.

The Goddess Indigo: I was very self-conscious of how I looked, back then; I thought I was not attractive enough. Anyhow, after that he blew into our community like a monsoon. All of a sudden everyone was talking about him. He was going by the name "Corwin" at the time, and became a fetish photographer: "Photos by Corwin". All I thought was, "Oh, it's the swinging guy." And then suddenly he was full-blown Leather. We met each other again because we were both going to MAsT Austin, and ironically we're now both the directors of that chapter.

Dr. Bob Rubel: The MAsT groups met in her home, so we were seeing each other once a month for years.

The Goddess Indigo: Years! I've been a guest at his online dinners, I've been a presenter at events we had both attended, and we always hit it off well. I was actually his realtor when he moved from one location to another, so we had all these connections. In the MAsT meetings, one of us would speak, and the other one would say, "Ah!" and furiously write. We even resonated with each other then, but it never crossed our minds to be together. That changed when his relationship with his previous master was dissolved. He had been organizing a formal Leather dinner for his MAsT chapter where he was in charge of the service and she was sitting opposite the MAsT director, Señor Jaime, at table.

Dr. Bob Rubel: My former Master and I were in New Orleans presenting at a conference, and during the presentation our relationship ended. We still managed to drive home together, but she said that she wasn't going to come the following weekend for the MAST dinner, because she didn't want people to think that we were still together. That left me four days to solve the problem.

The Goddess Indigo: I was dancing at a charity function with Dr. V that Señor Jaime was playing, and we were jamming out to the Hip-Shakin' Mamas—his band—and his slave V got a text and said, "Bob's relationship just ended! And they're supposed to be doing the dinner on Friday! Would you be willing to step in?" I said, "Of course! It's Bob!" So she messaged him and asked if he would be OK with the Goddess Indigo taking her place, and his answer was …

Dr. Bob Rubel: Is the Pope Catholic?

The Goddess Indigo: We agreed to meet ahead of time to discuss what protocols I would have in place that he would need to know about, how we could work together and feel simpatico. The meeting was at a Panera Bread—talk about an innocuous beginning— and it was magical. We made sense to each other, even then. We were seamless in coming together for the dinner. He asked me whether he should meet me at the place the formal dinner was being held, and I said, "No, this is formal. You will come pick me up." So he came and got me, and we had the most amazing conversation in the car on the way there, we continued it on the way back from the dinner, and we've been continuing that same conversation ever since.

In terms of his neurology; I am very good at compartmentalizing, so I understand his little boxes, very precise in size, where he drops his individual relationships and interactions, and also how he needs a recipe for success—how to move, how to behave. So he has created his own universe at his home where the same behaviors are required at all times. That level of what looks like formality to us, in my opinion, feels like safety to him. One thing that happens when boy is off kilter is that he becomes reactive. When that happens, he has such great remorse and regret afterwards, so what he's doing is trying to set up an environment where he can be loving and giving and gracious, and express himself as fully as possible, and create connections that he can actually feel.

As his master, I think I have a decent idea of what that means, and how to help him extrapolate that into going to conferences and moving in circles he's not familiar with. I've become really good at doing temperature checks with him. We'll be presenting a class and I'll say, "Hey, boy, you need to put on your jacket,", and he'll ask, "Why, Master?" And I'll say, "Because you're cold." And he won't even have noticed. In the beginning it used to floor him, but I've learned to note his physical signals and his level of discomfort, either emotionally, psychologically, or physically. I'm able to fill in and create that safe environment, even in places which are unfamiliar to him, which is where he starts to get edgy. Being with me helps him to feel less edgy, because he knows that I take care of most things.

We have never had an argument. We've been in a dynamic for almost five years, I've known him for almost twenty years, and we've never had one yet. We are both heavy believers in over-communicating, and our value systems line up very well. They're not identical, but we've worked out ways for them to be simpatico. In those ways, I believe I am a benefit to him. I understand enough of how his brain works, and what sets him off, that I'm able to stop that from happening. He's never been reactive with me the way he has been with others. Considering the amount and the length of time that we spend together, I think that's unusual.

Dr. Bob Rubel: It's unusual to find two people who think as similarly as you and I do, and who have such a similar breadth of information in our preferred fields. And no, I don't get reactive with you at all, and I generally don't with babygirl either. Bottom line is, I'm an introvert, and I try to avoid most social situations, because the chances are that I'm going to fuck up the interaction. I don't always handle it well. For example, I care quite a bit about where I am eating, and if I'm not eating at a pretty nice place, that's going to put me on edge. I eat the way I have eaten all my life. By the time I was in my mid-forties, every night has been a dress dinner.

The Goddess Indigo: I will say also that boy has picked up so many skills over the years! I've never met anyone who has transformed himself the way he has. I have so much respect for him and what he has accomplished in removing the traits that he thinks are holding him back, and replacing them with things he feels will be meaningful to his partners and enrich his life. It's mind-blowing. So in all honesty, I'm just enraptured. This is one of the most romantic relationships I've ever had. I love and cherish him very, very much. He is a gift.

When it comes to areas of concern, I think that one of my primary jobs is to set him up for success, and that means removing the stressors that would cause reactivity in him. I move very well socially, and when we are in public and he says something which may not be taken appropriately, I know how to smooth those things out. He's more relaxed with me because he knows I've got his back.

Also, because he can be non-reactive to what other people would consider criticism, I can be very blunt with him. At this point in our culture, it's important that when we present together, we don't use binary terms. So I can say, "At the last workshop, boy, you were using male-master and female-slave terms, and that is not going to fly." We can just work together on it, and I know his intentions are excellent. It's just that he's got ingrained and indoctrinated behaviors. But I don't have to couch it carefully. He takes it as constructive criticism and moves actively into alignment, which is just beautiful.

It took six months for us to figure out if we could work together, and one of the things I was looking for was malleability. I needed that because we do think differently sometimes; we see time differently, for example. I'm more of what we'd call a stew-maker—a pinch of this, a dash of that. He's a recipe-follower, a cake-maker type of person. He needs a recipe for success, not just throwing in a dash of this and that and we'll see what it tastes like. My type of mastery causes a bit more chaos for him—well, a lot more chaos if I'm being honest—so I needed to know that he had the resilience to handle my decision-making process, that the formula could change. I realized, working together during those six months, that even though changing direction wasn't easy for him, his intention was always to follow. So the malleability was there if I could guide it, and it's been beautiful. He's learned more about being less rigid since we've been together, and he has more trust in me than he has had in previous dynamics. We speak the same language, and I have enough depth and breadth of knowledge, and passion for what it is that we do, that he can place himself in my hands.

Dr. Bob Rubel: What makes Master so different from others is that she is competent across the board. There are people who are competent in their specialty. She's competent horizontally, not just vertically.

The Goddess Indigo: That is the most romantic thing that he has ever said to me, and every time he says it, I know what it means. And we problem-solve really well together. He'd locked himself out of his office the other day, and it took us a while to figure it out, but I found it interesting to see us working together. I was at my home, and he was locked out of his office at his home. He'd had a new door lock installed, and it turned out to be defective, so we worked together to unlock it from the exterior. It was like a logic problem. His phone, laptop, wallet and keys were all in the office. But one of the first things I did was to make him memorize my phone number; that was really important to me. He did contact me, and I was able to get into his house remotely through his security system to speak with him and figure out what to do.

When we're writing together or working together, there are times when we just stop and look at each other and start crying. It is so passionate and so miraculous. On the other hand, removing the emotional charge allows us to look at things very logically. That's something I do anyway, and having a partner who does the same is great. If there is reactivity, we know how to back away and say, "You know what? We need to look at this with a little more distance," and then we attack the problem.

I've shown him my method for problem-solving with a partner, which is "The problem is out there, it's never us," and he took to it immediately. We are always a team, and that is what made us successful—he enveloped me into his team rather than me being a separate person. When there's an issue, he comes to me and we solve it together; I don't pontificate from on high. His desire for alignment and his capacity to make that happen—for him, that's a logic problem and there's not an emotional charge, it's not ego-driven ... because he's on the spectrum. He just wants to get to that goal, and that makes life very simple. I don't attach a lot of emotions to us not reaching a goal, and I don't have a lot of expectations other than that we continue to move forward.

Also, I am what we call a visionary leader, but with that comes some baggage. I'm not good at follow-through, but boy is. He comes in and does the management portion and pulls us in the direction, while I provide the motivation, and pepper it with the inspiration and elbow grease to get us there. So our positions are very clear, and him being on the spectrum keeps us in those roles much better. He is more comfortable when we are well-seated in those roles.

Dr. Bob Rubel: I can't imagine not being in that role with Master.

The Goddess Indigo: Exactly! For us, it's who we are. Other people may see it as "I am Master at the moment"—no. This is who we see ourselves as at all times. Right before we came to this interview, I called him to see if it was the same link we'd used before. He answered the phone very casually and said, "Hey, what's up?' And I said, "Excuse me?" He asked, "What do you mean?" and I answered, "When do you talk like this?" He said, "I always answer the phone like this." I pointed out, "At this point there's been seven sentences and I've not heard a 'Master'." And he cried, "Oh! I thought that you were my sister!"

Dr. Bob Rubel: My sister had just hung up; we were in the middle of something, so I thought it was her.

The Goddess Indigo: I was completely thrown off balance, because that has never happened! We are always Master and boy. For the moment, I didn't know what to do with myself! But that formality means that he doesn't have to deal with me emotionally.

Dr. Bob Rubel: That's right. She actually keeps that from me. And I know what she's doing, and it makes perfect sense.

The Goddess Indigo: If I'm going through something, we actually have protocols in place where I remove myself, and I limit my contact while I work through it, because it's just going to muddy the waters and I'm not going to be as competent emotionally as he needs me to be. So he continues to "move as if" until I can return one hundred percent. I do have other sources of support that I pull in during those times—I have an extensive Leather family, and they are a great support to me.

If I were to give advice to a potential Master who is considering someone on the spectrum, I would say that for me it's not very different from any other type of dynamic that I might put together. When everyone is willing, no one is the enemy. You do the research necessary to make your relationship succeed. No man is an island unto themselves, so you need support. What does that look like? Therapy? Family? Whatever it is, go out there and get it. Make sure that you have the tools in your toolbag to make the relationship work.

Because someone is different doesn't make anyone more right or more wrong. Our differences are what make our world magical, and take us away from the mundane. So find ways to embrace them. For me, boy being on the spectrum is a superpower, not a disability by any stretch of the imagination. The more I understand and the more I can support him, the stronger we are. Remember that we're all on the same team, we want the best for each other, and we mean each other no harm. If we can really do that and mean that and feel that, then the rest is up to you.

Dr. Bob Rubel: I'm not really a submissive; I'm a subordinate. I'm a dominant in service, and the readers have to be sophisticated enough to make that distinction. I would say that it's important for both parties to familiarize themselves with the characteristics of what's referred to as Level 1 autism. Those characteristics are virtually me. I also recommend that both parties take a bevy of tests for personality and characteristics, such as Myers-Briggs, Kolbe A, love languages tests, stress tests, etc. Compare the results. We have found it extremely helpful to know where Master sits and where I sit and where babygirl sits—for example, babygirl is an extrovert and the two of us are introverts, but Master is more extroverted than I am; I don't leave the house if I can help it, and I rarely interact with people. We do not have people over for dinner. The older I get, the worse it is.

Therapy is always very good, because the more you understand yourself, the more information you can offer your partner. Understand how the other person takes in information, and how they think. The greatest problem I had in my first marriage was that I couldn't understand how my wife of seventeen years thought, and our problem-solving skills were so far apart that I finally couldn't stand it and left. Master is the first person I've been able to surrender to.

We deal a lot in the concept of alignment, so if anything goes off kilter on my side, she'll comment. "I think we're out of alignment on this one, boy." Then we can figure it out. Master thinks faster than I do, which is always a delight. The way I used to explain myself is that I was born without common sense. I have other kinds of sense, but I just do not have pragmatic common sense. If I can say the wrong thing, chances are that I'll end up doing it, and Master is extremely good at guiding me in those areas.

The Goddess Indigo: When I notice, during a public conversation, that boy is on edge, I'll be reaching out to him after the conversation to find out what's going on. I'll talk it out with him, which tends to help put things into perspective for him as well. So when I see the signs that he's a little on edge, we'll be working on that together. But I am aware that he is one hundred per-cent capable of doing what needs to be done in the moment, and that we can take care of it later.

Dr. Bob Rubel: And I won't notice it. I won't feel on edge.

The Goddess Indigo: That is correct—prior to me, he wouldn't notice he was on edge until he had exploded. When I see signs that he is on edge, I ask him what's going on. He has to stop and evaluate whether anything happened that he may be carrying around. When he figures it out, we'll start working on it; it's an unraveling that needs to happen. It's a process, but we both enjoy it, and when we're done we feel triumphant. We accepted the challenge together and we solved the puzzle! We both like that. And then we keep moving.

We took those first six months to make sure that what we had could be sustainable. There are M-types who just want to take care of someone, and that's fine if you find the right partner. But only having energy in one direction doesn't work well, so finding ways that we could feed each other was important. It was also important that I was competent to be his master. Just because he is an incredibly intelligent and adorable man doesn't mean that he has to be mine. If I can't set him, myself, and our dynamic up for success, then I don't need to take it on. We need to be able to look at ourselves with pragmatism, and figure out if we're tall enough to ride this ride. That's incredibly important. The trust that we evoke in each other can make the solution traumatic for both parties, so knowing that you're big enough for the ride is crucial.

Masters on the Spectrum

Mastery Without a Mask
Cassidy Laurens

I didn't know I was autistic or ADHD until I was in my mid-40's. I was living life in "hard mode" and didn't know it, silently struggling to learn, to function, and to socialize, all while wondering why everything seemed so simple for everyone else. I survived by devoting myself to people-pleasing and bending to every other person's whim, desire, or expectation, all while maintaining my meticulously constructed mask (i.e. un/conscious camouflaging of autistic traits to appear neurotypical). Having been socialized as a woman, that was all I knew. *Be pleasant. Smile. Stand by your man. Do as you're told.*

I had been living abroad in Scotland and was nearly a year into my PhD when my world crumbled. I was in chronic autistic burnout with decades of accumulated trauma when I crashed and burned. After recounting my struggles in school, a friend suggested I might be ADHD. I arranged an evaluation through my university's student disability service and was also identified as autistic, which was enough to gain access to academic accommodations. It was a further two years on a waitlist before my formal psychiatric diagnoses, often required to access health or government-based disability services.

An autism diagnosis in adults takes precedence over other (not so) minor learning disabilities. While not formally diagnosed, I also struggle with significant auditory processing disorder (slow processing/comprehension for what I hear, especially language and speech).

Despite many who would describe me as articulate, writing and speaking are areas where I have low aptitude but hard-won skills. I am a visual thinker with hyperphantasia (movie-like visualization) and visual synesthesia (e.g., seeing sound and music). Language is not my primary operating system and I have no internal monologue. Every thought or emotion, all communication must be translated from imagery into language for me to express myself. When low on spoons (a measure of capacity commonly used in chronic illness communities) or in autistic burnout, I lose speech and language skills (a.k.a. situational mutism).

Now let me tell you why this backstory matters. I've always known I was kinky, long before I knew what it meant or how it often overlaps with sexuality. I came out to BDSM and Leather in my early twenties as a submissive. Considering my socialized gender, masking, and people-pleasing, it never occurred to me to be anything different. I thought that being a cute, femme, flexible bottom who never complained was what I was supposed to do. There were a few who saw something in me and began training me as a Dominant, but without knowing myself behind the mask, I was unable to consistently connect to my own inner D-type. It was simpler to submit.

I took this dysfunctional behavior to the extreme and became a slave, thinking that if I could just keep one person (an Owner) happy then maybe I wouldn't feel like I had to people-please with everyone else. There were also many aspects of M/s dynamics which were attractive to me: consciously created structure, clear expectations for behavior, protocols I could learn, and routines that soothed my autistic brain and need for consistency and stability.

Unfortunately, I was coerced into M/s by my former abusive partner when he decided he wanted a slave and told me that if I couldn't do it, he would leave me. Sadly, a history of trauma and abuse are common for autistics. To explain this high incidence of abuse in autistic populations, the current thought is that the apparent "lack of social skills" prevents an autistic from correctly reading the situation. I believe instead that my fear of being ostracized, shame at being different, heavy masking, and extreme people-pleasing meant that I was unable to know what was best for me or to stand up for myself. My narcissistic sociopath of an ex saw me as easy prey. (As they do.)

Most people in the community naturally perceived me as a slave for many years after that relationship ended. I internalized that identity because that's what was being mirrored back to me. I tried desperately to be a slave, but it never worked. I would start a new dynamic on my best pleasing (masked) behavior, and then once I got comfortable, I would drop the mask. Those poor D- and M-types probably thought that I suddenly became a different person and that was not what they signed up for. Eventually I gave up and backed away from the M/s community and from power dynamics to focus on other communities and kinks.

Being diagnosed as an adult was lifechanging in the best way, but it took some time to integrate. The single greatest realization after my dual diagnoses was that I wasn't a broken neurotypical, I was autistic. I learned that there was nothing at all wrong with my brain, but it did work differently than allistic (non-autistic) or neurotypical brains. I began the long process of integrating this new information, educating myself about my neurotype, joining online neurodivergent communities, and getting to know the person I had unknowingly been suppressing. It took some time to learn how to best work with my brain instead of against it. Essential to this process was naming, owning, and enforcing my communication and sensory needs and learning that I was in control of my environment. After a lifetime of prioritizing everyone else's feelings and putting myself on the bottom rung of the social ladder, I finally felt empowered to give myself the validation that I had been seeking externally my whole life. With practice expressing this internally and at home, it was an easy jump to realize that I wanted to express that same power in my intimate relationships and sex/kink life. I started Dominating again and haven't looked back. As it turns out, I do, in fact, know what I am doing, and I'm not too bad at this thing that we do.

It's commonly known that autistics might be drawn to power exchange or Authority Transfer dynamics because of the predictable structure and clarity in rules and expectations. For my M/s dynamic, I loved establishing the relationship structure, creating a process for communication and feedback, and inventing protocols for my slave to follow. M/s gives me structure and predictability amid the ambiguity of human social interaction. For my autistic brain, routine means fewer spoons and a greater sense of safety. There is a sense of absoluteness to an M/s dynamic. I know how the relationship works because I designed it that way. I make the final decisions and that's rarely, if ever, questioned. This surety is a balm to my active, busy autistic brain.

I met my first slave during the time between being identified autistic/ADHD (AuDHD in some communities because the dual diagnosis is so common) but before formal diagnoses. I had been playing as a Dominant regularly, connecting with this newly identified self within, and getting practice exerting the control I needed and wanted in my relationships. When we began to discuss potential Ownership, I knew I had to tell it that I was autistic. My internal acceptance process was still new and tender, and I felt some embarrassment when I came out to it. Luckily, my (neurotypical) slave was wonderful and accepting. it explained that it didn't care and that it sees me as a person, not a collection of traits or diagnoses. It had already decided that it wished to seek Ownership with me, and the fact that I had a name for some traits didn't make any difference to it.

Once I got past my own internal need for peer approval, I was able to step fully into my proverbial Master's boots, as well as my literal Muir cap. There was no M/s community where I was living at the time to offer support or a mirror, but I had been gifted my cap in a formal recognition ceremony more than thirteen years before. All I needed to do was to claim it as my own, and after some deep introspection and reevaluation, I did.

If I take any mental breaks from reveling in Ownership, Mastery, and Dominance, it might be to express some sadness and grief at the lost time before my diagnoses when I did not know myself. I feel a joy and deep sense of rightness and completion when Dominating and Mastering. There are few things in my experience that have "clicked" for me like consensually expressing my Authority in my personal relationships.

Like many neurodivergent people, I struggle with executive dysfunction. ADHD meds improve focus, but they are not a fix-all. Shouldering the responsibility for my slave or sub's wellbeing within a scene, dynamic, or relationship gives me a source of external motivation. I show up for them, cultivate mental/physical health, commit to best practices, and put myself first. I know I deserve my best, but it feels easier for me with the additional accountability of a slave or sub in my life. I like myself more when I have someone in my care.

Luckily kink, BDSM, Leather, and Authority Exchange/power dynamics are a special interest for me, and I rarely have difficulty engaging my interest-based focus for play or dynamics. It feeds my autistic brain to delve deep into philosophical rabbit holes or to collect all the details for a new skill I wish to add to my repertoire. As luck would have it, neurodiversity is also a special interest of mine.

Authority-based BDSM play has also been beneficial, especially to my various sensory needs. While my primary "love language" is touch, I am touch-averse without consent or pre-negotiated approval. Playing with physical restraint, a personal favorite, allows me to choose when I want touch and how I receive it. If my brain is weary of words or conversation, then I can hood my slave and "poof!—it becomes an ottoman. Provided I consider the basic needs of the property, of course, my needs and wants are paramount whether they are cognitive, sexual, physical, or neurological. I find this style of dynamic intensely rewarding and validating.

The ADHD aspect of my brain, however, craves novelty. With my interest-based attention, I tend to hyperfocus during play, a sensation that I am told can be delightfully intense and even addictive. I tend to shut out the surrounding environment and am intensely aware of my bottom's body, their breathing, their reactions, and their subtle movements and sounds. BDSM play that is different every time gives me the new and novel stimulation that ADHD-brain requires. Having multiple partners also keeps play fresh with new influxes of ideas, fantasies, and changing wants and needs. I have learned a great deal about myself and my bottoms from each of my dynamics.

My slave, who is British and lives in the UK, is a neurotypical cisgender man. When asked for its perspective on our dynamic for a class I was putting together on neurodiversity and M/s, it expressed some discomfort with my desire to dissect or analyze my traits because it believed that its only role was to be obedient; it believes my neurotype was probably the reason that when we met it perceived my Dominance as different or "on another level" compared to its past experience. My slave noted that I often missed its subtle hints or suggestions, which forced it to either release its expectations for its own desires or to explicitly ask me for what it wanted; it felt that its submission was enforced and intensified since it knows it cannot be devious. (Not that it would do that anyway.)

My slave enjoys my attention to detail because I take notes and keep records, but also because of my mental storage capacity; it likes that I don't let things slip and I provide reminders. My slave also likes it must keep up with me, because it knows I will not forget; it might casually mention an interest or play idea when horny during a conversation, and the next thing it knows I've integrated its fantasy into a scene. My slave deeply appreciates that I enjoy meticulously planning my scenes and that I have a framework and know the directions in which I want to push it. To me, this feels normal. If I have a plan, then I make sure the toys are clean and to hand, and I have a direction and intention for my scenarios. I may also shift with little notice and enjoy working intuitively in the moment, but I like having a place to start. My slave has enjoyed my hyperfocus, persistence, and stamina for play, which has offered it an opportunity to rise to my demands and to please me.

One challenge we had around our play is that my slave really craved and enjoyed verbal humiliation and degradation. When I am in my hyperfocus zone, I rarely speak more than is necessary, preferring communication based in physical contact (or lack thereof). My differences around language and speaking made incorporating verbal play a real challenge for me. Knowing this was important to it, I scripted some verbal scenarios much like I would for other social situations.

One other area that was a challenge for me was the banter (playful, good-humored teasing) and cheek (insolent or rude behavior or talk). Americans might equate "cheek" with being a "smart ass". I had to overcome some cultural barriers as an American living in Britain, as well as neurological differences—because I take things literally—to discern between banter/cheek and disobedience. I think the slave also learned to be very careful giving me cheek, just in case I didn't take it with the good humor with which it was intended.

I have used our protocols to stabilize my own routines. For example, when we were living in the same time zone its required goodnight message was my signal to switch gears and start to wind down for the night. As a chronic insomniac, any external support I can find that helps me sleep is beneficial. Now that we are an ocean apart, its good morning messages are often my signal that I should have been in bed an hour before.

Having settled somewhat into this absoluteness of Ownership with my slave, I stumbled a bit moving back to the States and reorienting to new D/s dynamics after adding two amazing submissive partners to my life. They have been very patient while I sorted out the differences in my own mind between my Owning or training a slave and establishing an ongoing dynamic with submissive partners who are not mine to Own. I've had to adapt to a lot more relationship ambiguity, next to no Authority, and only temporary control. Gratefully, I have also found two extraordinary collaborators, both of whom are neurodivergent. And they are friends with each other, thank the gods, which makes communication in our polyamorous lives a lot smoother.

In conversations with both subs in preparation for this essay, we all expressed a deep gratitude for feeling seen as precisely who we are. In both relationships there is helpful mirroring for functioning, coping, sensory, and communication differences. They have both described a comfort in discovering that I am a person to whom they do not have to explain their broad neurodivergences, only the individual specifics. One partner likened this effect to a trans person having sex with another trans person for the first time. There exists an automatic shorthand for communication and a similar language and comprehension which we have all found extremely validating.

Something else I intuitively understand is what it was like growing up and walking through the world being bombarded with negative talk from parents, teachers, or classmates. *You're so smart, what's wrong with you? If only you applied yourself, you could get good grades and get into a good college. Why can't you do what I ask and clean your room? You're so weird* (complete with look of disgust). *Look at me when I'm talking to you. Just pay attention!* It's no surprise that unsupported neurodivergent kids grow up to be anxious, depressed, and often traumatized adults who easily fall into a cycle of self-blame and low self-worth. Throw in healthy doses of queerness, aspec (a/sexual/romantic spectrum), or gender nonconformity and it's a recipe for a lifetime of dysfunctional relationships and mental health challenges.

As a Dominant, I offer opportunities for success when assigning tasks or service, giving orders, or training for desired behavior. When correction or critique has been required, I interrupt the self-blame cycle, if necessary, and then give another chance for them to improve. I am enthusiastic with my praise and am open to adapting any rules that aren't working. Three of my basic rules for any s-type are:

❖ If I have not told you how I want something done, then you cannot do it wrong, only not my way.
❖ It is my responsibility to teach you how to serve me. It is yours to learn and remember.
❖ I expect your best effort, not perfection.

With any neurodivergent dynamic, a broad knowledge base about neurodiversity is key to understanding and empathy. I recommend a high level of patience with the individual and setting a slow pace to learn each other's idiosyncrasies. ADHD/executive function coaching tips have proven invaluable to me getting what I want and need in my dynamics with the least amount of distress, shame, or self-blame.

With neurodivergent s-types, it's even more important to focus on their strengths and to meet them where they are. What is easy for one is not easy for all. I once had a sub with dyspraxia who had a difficult time helping me on and off with my lace-up Doc Martens because he couldn't tie a bow. Instead, I had him help with getting my feet in or out and I managed the laces, making sure we both got something we wanted. I've also had a lot of success by allowing for self-discovery through suggestion. Rather than assigning a task, I toss out something I want to know during a discussion to see if it gets picked up. My smart and infinitely capable s-types have amazed me sometimes with what they come back to me with when I give them latitude to apply themselves.

I don't expect to always have my sub's full attention (or eye contact) unless I remove all distractions or provide sufficient intense sensation to direct focus in the moment. I allow space for distracting thoughts (affectionately called "Roomba-brain") and feelings, and if need be, I will direct their attention and focus back to the present moment. (Sometimes I will even do it gently.) I have chosen to provide more frequent reminders where there has been difficulty remembering orders, rules, or protocols, and am more lenient with consequences. Effort matters too, not only results.

With both submissive partners, I have felt seen and heard, and better able to express my own unique challenges. I will sometimes struggle with emotional dysregulation, and both subs have joyfully offered me emotional labor when I might have otherwise kept my internal process to myself. I am learning to trust that my multitude of idiosyncrasies are just as welcome in our shared space as theirs. I am as grateful as they are for the ease of communication, the shorthand language, the acceptance of oddball interests, and the external motivation.

One sub, F, is a genderqueer transman with ADHD. Like many queers, he's had friends and lovers who are on the spectrum, but this is his first dynamic with an autistic D-type. He is still learning how I operate and adjusting his expectations to my capacity. I'm an introvert with limited social spoons and have a fair number of years on him. He is an exuberant, excitable puppy and an extrovert who craves social contact. He admits it's been a challenge to not blame himself when we stumble across a mismatch in needs, but he appreciates the more active process around negotiations than he's had before. He's found some peace in knowing that what I do offer is what I want to be giving.

F has enjoyed watching me mask less while also juggling multiple dynamics and working to know myself. He also appreciates that I have a similar trauma history. F feels grateful for the validation and sanity check about patterns that I notice as a D-type, but also as a friend and comrade who wants to see him well and healthy. *"It's pretty damned incredible and not something I expected."*-F

F and I enjoy our "Roomba-brain" conversations where it's all in the flow and we manage to help each other remember some of the loose tangential threads until it circles around again to where we began.

One of my favorite things to do with him is to engage the interest-based attention, redirect it where I want it by controlling the conversation, and then to shut it down and "force" his attention to be here now. He deeply appreciates the clarity of the present moment and the opportunity to know that he is precisely where I want him to be.

We're going to be working soon on some shame-free accountability practice together. He will come up with some ideas of what he wants to improve, such as meal prep or organization, and I will offer reminders or check-ins as necessary to make sure he stays on track. If a task gets missed, I will mention it without blame and ask what could be done differently for the next time.

My other submissive partner, A, is nonbinary, queer, greysexual, autistic, and ADHD. They aren't formally diagnosed, but being in a dynamic with me has been super validating as they have many opportunities to see how similar, and different, our minds can be when interacting with the world. We followed each other on social media for a few years and had friends in common, but when we finally had an opportunity to connect in person it was immediately apparent to me that they were a kindred spirit. We are eerily similar in some ways, but also delightfully opposite, especially when it comes to D/s and kink. For two autistic humans, discovering that we share some of our special interests has been a unique joy and source of amusement … and endless Star Trek memes.

In our dynamic, A has felt seen in novel ways. They have had dynamics with others who've not understood that they don't multitask well, get overwhelmed with certain types of attention or focus, or that they have no sense of unverbalized social or relationship expectations. With me, they have had remarkable catharsis around some of those previous relationships. From the beginning there has been a feeling of safety and vulnerability between us that I suspect has been enhanced by our similar communication styles and sensory needs.

> I've found my time with Cassidy to be immensely comforting. I know where I stand … err, kneel … with them. And they make a great deal of space to talk and communicate things through, and it's thorough and insightful. We both tend to have rich inner worlds and communicating them takes time, and we both seem to make time for

each other sharing it. Everything has seemed like an asset in terms of communicating. Taking our time, figuring out what we each mean when we talk about things, learning stories and nuances.   – A

One thing that we both have made a priority is respecting and supporting each other's needs for consistency and routine. Keeping to a schedule for our regular time together has benefitted both of us, and communicating potential changes early helps to mitigate anxiety around uncertainty and change. Because our protocols and rituals are built on things that give us both pleasure, we find them stabilizing and they serve us both by creating predictability and safety.

There have been some interesting challenges around making rituals happen. Frequent verbal reminders have been helpful, but we recently discovered a physical stimulus was even better. One day they forgot to take off my boots after our usual greeting ritual. I let it go, took off my own boots, and sat down to think about it. When I voiced my disappointment, they explained that every time before when they helped me on or off with my boots I was sitting down. That was the system. So now I sit, they remember to help with my boots without being prompted, and we both get what we want. The system could be changed, of course, but finding a way to work within an already established system or routine is far more efficient.

Executive functioning support has become a regular part of our dynamic. On a particularly distractible day, I might work with them to remember all the complex steps to a task by asking questions like "Don't the vegetables need to go into the oven first?" In exchange, I get a delicious and healthy dinner cooked for me. I also tend to remember where they put their glasses or phone, and often have an answer to the "Now where was I, what was I doing?" questions. This work requires carrying an immense mental load, but I find great joy in it. I have a highly organized, systems-oriented brain that sees twelve steps ahead in any given moment, so management of this nature feels natural. It's a relief to express it in healthy, consensual, and helpful ways.

On the opposite end of the spectrum of executive functioning support is the ability to step back and get out of their way. If my basic desire is for a cup of coffee, I am delighted when they dive into it with enthusiasm and develop their own system that works best for them. I don't have a desire to control how the coffee is made, only that I receive it in a timely manner. I suspect if I tried to micromanage this task, it would be deeply challenging to them, and I wouldn't get as good a cup of coffee. The difficult part is discerning when to offer support, and when to let them run with it.

A also experiences demand avoidance, which is not uncommon to autistics. Like executive dysfunction, it's their brain absolutely refusing to do the thing and not just being stubborn or noncompliant. Even for someone wired for service, submission, and obedience, if they hear an order given in an authoritative tone, they experience immediate resistance. They doubt that I would be able to navigate this if I weren't neurodivergent myself and feel that it gives me an advantage in working with their brain.

I recognized this in A early in our relationship, but it took me some time to figure out the best way to handle it while still getting what I want. Facing demand avoidance head on tends to escalate the resistance. Instead, I've learned to sidestep it by using requests (Will you please fix me a cup of coffee?), by making statements about what would please me (I would like a cup of coffee), and through collaboration. When I wanted an end of scene ritual where they thank me for my efforts, I asked them for their ideas. As luck would have it, their idea was precisely what I had in mind. We both got something we needed.

One last aspect to a dynamic with an autistic human that needs to be discussed is that of sensory processing and sensory overwhelm. Autistics can be sensory seeking (stimming), or sensory avoidant. The needs/desires/perception of a given sensory input can also vary day to day based on capacity. Sensory input, when calculating for overwhelm or shutdown, is cumulative. Reducing sight or sound often means more capacity to process physical or emotional sensations of a scene. As the D-type, I'm able to manage most of my own sensory overwhelm by not playing at all if the space is too busy or the music too loud, by changing my plans for a scene, or leaving a party if it gets to be too much. Aftercare for me often means quiet time away from people.

A is known in the community as a heavy masochist with a remarkable capacity for pain processing. But that's on a good day, when they feel comfortable expressing that aspect of themselves, or feel a need for that type of sensation. Their interest in and capacity for intense vs gentle sensation changes from day to day. Due to the nature of our dynamic, my ability to read them, and the work we have both put in to establish safety and trust, we have been able to play with many forms of masochism besides intense sensation, including consensual sensory overwhelm.

Let me caution that if you are only just starting to play with an autistic bottom, sensory overwhelm is a thing to avoid. It can lead to shutdowns, meltdowns, panic attacks, or dissociation, and the bottom may never want to play with that sensation, or you, ever again. When used consciously, cautiously, and with careful negotiation akin to that of consensual non-consent (CNC), it can be a powerful tool for control and surrender.

It has taken many months of careful practice to begin to use this tool. First there was mapping their physical body, learning the places where intense sensation was welcome and where it was not, much like I would do for any bottom. Then there was learning the places, sensations, and activities that they deeply enjoyed but that could easily cause overwhelm and shutdown. That's the realm of sensory overwhelm edgeplay. My intense hyperfocus during play has been helpful in staying alert and learning how to walk these edges, because sensory overwhelm can come up without much warning. If I don't give them a break from the sensation, or switch to something else, they can be over that edge in a blink. End of scene.

Sensory deprivation has also been an extremely useful tool for us. Aside from being a personal favorite for fun and fetish, we have used hoods, blindfolds, and earplugs to consciously reduce sensory input. During one scene at a play party using gentler sensations, a blindfold and earplugs helped them to focus and enjoy the scene much more because they didn't have to process the sounds of other scenes or bright lights. In that situation, I was not using lack of sight or sound to my advantage as the Dominant, which is the difference between using the tool for play and using it to help manage sensory overwhelm.

Much like our use of sensory deprivation, compression has been both a fun activity during a scene and a tool for regulation. We have used weighted blankets and sandbags, but compression for us usually means that I sit or more often lie on top of them using my full body weight. We find this to be a sweet and connecting time, although I have threatened to use them as a mattress one day and fall asleep there. A has also served me as a regulation aid when I am struggling. Their quiet, calm presence kneeling before me with their head in my lap has become one of my favorite neurological homeostasis tools. We both come away from those moments feeling grounded and more connected.

The most important skills when playing with any neurodivergent bottom or submissive, or Dominant/Master for that matter, are self-awareness, consent, and communication. We must know ourselves well enough to communicate our idiosyncratic needs, to manage our own spoons and shifting capacities, and to trust our partners to meet us where we are. That might mean my slave's graceful acceptance, the rambling tangential conversations I have with F, or the special-interest-sharing, safe space in my dynamic with A.

I am deeply grateful for the love I have received from each one of my s-types who, simply by being a part of my life, help me to learn and grow. I still live life in "hard mode", but now I can better identify and communicate my needs. When those needs are met with curiosity and enthusiasm instead of negativity and shame, I feel validated and supported in expressing my Dominance and Mastery without a mask.

Cassidy is a queer, polyamorous, AFAB, nonbinary, autistic, and ADHD human who lives with chronic illness and enjoys exerting Authority, Dominance, and Mastery in their intimate relationship dynamics. They have been active in the BDSM and Leather scenes for more than half their life in the US and the UK and hold the past title of International Ms. Leather 2007. Cassidy owns one slave and has two submissive neurodivergent partners. They hold a doctorate in biological anthropology and currently reside in the San Francisco Bay Area.

Interview with Master Penguin and slave ginna

Master Penguin: So slave ginna and I have been together for twenty-six years, married twenty-five of those. We've had an M/s relationship for somewhere around twenty-something years—I don't know for sure; we never had an official date for it, so it's hard to pin that down. She struggled with the word "slave" for a while, so she was fighting defining the relationship in this way as well. When it exactly happened is really kind of murky, but we've been involved in the BDSM community at large since at least 2001, and we started moving in M/s circles around 2010.

Slave ginna: We were always kinky from the time we first started dating each other, and it was a gradual evolution from there. I think because we're both neurodivergent—I have ADHD and my own idiosyncrasies as well—the M/s dynamic shift came more naturally for us because of the structure and routines and that sort of thing. It made it easier for us to move into this 24/7. But there was no specific date, no collaring ceremony or anything like that.

Master Penguin: As far as my ASD is concerned … I never knew, as a child, that this was what I had. I always knew that there was something different about me, but I didn't have a name for it. That was back in the early '80s, and back then when you talked about autism, you meant something like Dustin Hoffman in *Rain Man*, and that looked quite different from the kind of autism I have. It's on the same spectrum, obviously, but it doesn't present in the same way. I always had little peculiarities in school, and I didn't pick up on how weird they looked to others. To me, it *was* normal; it was just my life, and it wasn't strange to me. But looking back, there was something not quite normal going on.

Eventually I found this lovely woman, and we got together and had kids, and my oldest child has autism as well. They actually diagnosed him very early on, around three or four, which is not average for autism; they usually want to wait until the kid is older. Early on, they had him on the drug-of-the-month club—"let's try this, or this, or this"—but eventually we stopped that, because it was causing more harm than good. When he got off all the medications, he became more normal—or whatever "normal" is for us. But as part of the journey of understanding what was going on with him, I kept going back and thinking, "Wait a minute. This all sounds very familiar. Where have I heard this before?" I had to do some soul-searching on my own, and once my son was diagnosed with Aspergers Syndrome, it became obvious to me that his father had it as well, and just never had the definition.

I was only officially diagnosed about eight years ago. I had circumstances at my job where I felt like I needed to protect myself—to cover myself ADA-wise—because my job was taking inbound phone calls for a company, and I was rated partly on how I sounded on the phone. Did I express the right emotion? Was I flat? And, of course, being ASD, that's a hallmark of some of the problems we have. I didn't have a terribly flat affect—I didn't sound like Ben Stein in *Ferris Bueller*—but there were times I felt like that in order for it to sound like I was having emotion, I had to exaggerate it in my speech. If I just spoke normally for myself, it came out in a flat monotone. I asked my co-workers, "Hey, does it sound like I'm faking it? Am I going over the top?" and they all said, "No, no, you sound completely normal." And I was thinking, "Phew, thank God, because I'm not. I'm really trying very hard." So that was how the diagnosis came about. I felt like I had to protect myself, because some of my performance reviews were starting to reflect it, and my scoring wasn't good enough. I needed to be able to say, "Hey guys, this is something I really can't control." I mean, I try, but it will never come naturally.

As far as the rest of my life ... well, yeah, I like my routines, I have a set pattern I like to go through. I'm not a big fan of surprises or last-minute changes. I like to think that over the years I've gotten better at ducking and weaving when necessary, when a sudden change comes up. I have sensory issues which manifest in different ways. A lot of them have to do with sudden or unexpected noises. I'll be sitting here in my chair doing something and I'll hear a sudden noise, and I'll yell through the house, "Hey, what is that sound?" As soon as I know what it is I'm OK, but if I can't quite put my finger on it, it drives me batty until I can actually identify it. I have problems with rough clothing, tastes, textures, all of that. But I've gotten more used to it over the years; it's not something I can control completely, but I've learned to cope with it as best I can.

Slave ginna: One thing that attracted me to him—because I have a trauma background—is that he was always brutally honest. Even before we had the diagnosis, I knew that if I asked him, "Does my hair look all right?" he would tell me straight out if there was a problem with my hair. That really built up the trust in our relationship, because I knew that what I saw was what I got, and there was nothing fake about him. That was very refreshing, because I knew he wasn't playing games with me. I'd met a lot of neurotypical people who wouldn't do that. He likes routines and structure, and that really meshed well with my idiosyncrasies. I have my own sensory issues from the ADHD as well, so that was something I could relate to.

Master Penguin: With Ginna's ADHD—and PTSD, but I'm speaking to the ADHD here—I do a lot of the planning as to when we go places or do things, because ADHD people have a notoriously bad concept of time. If we run on her time, it messes us up. So I'm the planner and the keeper of the schedules, and my ASD helps to pull that in line. She doesn't always like the time frame I'm keeping, but she's learned to live with that, because that's part of the give-and-take of what we do.

There are definitely times when I get fried or burnt out. If we're in a crowd and there's too much noise, sometimes I can't take it any more and I have to go to a quiet place; or if I'm dealing with people I may need to back off. I've gotten better at it over the years, but it's great that I have someone available to me who understands where I'm at and doesn't take it personally when I can't always be actively directing everything, or have to go into my cave and be a hermit for a while. She doesn't take offense at that because she knows that's what has to happen for me to recover.

Slave ginna: I learned early on that I had to spell things out for him; that he wasn't going to read my mind. Masters don't read minds anyway, but if I had a need as an s-type, I had to say, "OK, Master, I need this." That was a challenge for me because of my history, but it was also very good for me. Because I *had* to do that with him, it taught me to come out of my shell and advocate for myself.

Over the years I've been able to learn his "tells" for getting overwhelmed and overstimulated, especially when we're in crowds. I can ask him if he needs to go someplace and just chill out for a little bit. Sometimes communication can be a challenge—I'll say something to him and I'll think he heard it because he responded, but he may be somewhere else mentally. Also, I might say something and then I'll assume from the look on his face that he's mad at me, and I'll overreact. And it's not that he's mad, it's just that he's thinking about something. I had to learn that what's on his face doesn't necessarily match what's in his head. We've had to be really correct when it comes to talking about feelings, asking what someone is really feeling.

As far as the time thing: Sometimes we get in a feedback loop where he's waiting for me and I'm waiting for him, but neither of us have communicated it. So that can be a challenge sometimes.

Master Penguin: My slave is my universal translator. Her job is to be a buffer between me and the world. She handles a lot of the social media—as I said earlier, for a long time my job was to be on the phone, so when I got home I didn't particularly want to be on the telephone talking to people, because that was what I did for eight hours a day. If there are people we need to call or bills which need to be negotiated or a problem with service, I'm usually going to have her make those phone calls.

We have a calendar in the hallway where we have everyone's appointments, things we need to get to the store, anything to cope with the family's neurodivergence. Everyone has to pass it in order to get to bed. She coordinates the social media and planning for events. Right now we're in our title year, and she's the one reaching out to the chapters to pin down dates and times and topics. We may have discussions about it, but ninety-five per cent of the time she's the one who is sending messages to people in order to get the work done.

She's also an emotional support kitty, and she's there when I need it. If I'm overwhelmed she can help calm me down and get me back to where I need to be, and I definitely use that service whenever I need it.

Slave ginna: He sometimes has problems with scents or textures on his hands, and I know what to get in order to take care of that. I've worked over the years to find different grooming products for him that don't affect his sensory issues.

When it comes to our community, it's hard enough remembering who's with who, so if we're out and about I'll remind him, "This is that person, we met them at such-and-such a place—and oh, by the way, they're not with this person any more; they're now with this person." I'm better at keeping track of that, and I'm better at reading faces, so I can help if he has a question about whether that person seems angry with him or is just having a bad day. I can translate people for him. He implements the schedule, but I manage it, so I can warn him if there's going to be a change and he can prepare for it.

We're going to have to fly on a plane to the international Master/slave competition soon, and I'm already preparing for that. He might have a sensory problem, like his ears popping, or just too many people on the plane, and I'm looking for ways to buffer the trip so it won't be so much of a sensory overload experience for him. We're going in a day early so we can chill and relax. It's my job to think ahead and make his experience the best it can be.

Master Penguin: I'd like to say that we were preparing to run for the Northeast Master/slave title for ten years, but that's not exactly true because I had to drag her along for years and convince her that this was something we wanted to do. For myself, I'd been planning it for ten years. We started branching out about six years ago and doing presentations for different MAsT chapters, and we discussed what we wanted to talk about; what kind of classes did we want to teach? The two main subject areas we came up with were "How do you deal with sexual trauma in M/s?" and "How do you deal with neurodiversity in M/s?"

Then we looked at each other and asked, "Do we really want to be *those people?*" Where every time we walk in, people are going to be thinking, 'Oh, here they come, they're going to be talking about autism or sexual abuse again…'" Early on, we really thought it would be better to talk about other things. A couple of years after that, though, it became pretty obvious that there was a need out there. We needed to be talking about these issues, and showing representation for this. So we finally said, "Screw it, if that means we're *those people*, then OK. We'll hang our hat on that. We certainly have experience dealing with these things, so we might as well lean into it. We might as well—I don't want to say *be experts in it*, because we're not professionals, but we live it every day of our lives. We have perspectives and understanding and ideas and solutions as to how to cope with it better. We know we're not the only ones out there. So when we ran for Northeast, that set us apart, because we weren't just talking about hypotheticals. Our main presentation for the contest was on what we'd personally been told, and what we did to accommodate them in our dynamic. "This is what we did to counteract some of these supposed negatives and turn them positive, in order to have a more successful relationship." We thought about it together and decided to embrace it, because that's who we are. It made us more authentic as a couple, and that's what's important when we're out there representing. We are who we are, and we're not pretending to be somebody else.

Slave ginna: We've never really been the popular kids, so we don't necessarily care what other people think. Plus we're both too neurodivergent to fake it very easily, so we figured we would speak to what we knew. It really doesn't get talked about enough; a lot of neurodivergent people don't look like they have physical illnesses, so no one can see it right away, or figure out why they're acting like that—or reacting like that. So we felt it was needed. IF it could just help one person, it would be worth saying.

Honestly, I think that if we had a vanilla marriage, we would have broken up a long time ago, because of everything we've been through with our difficulties. Having the M/s component has forced us to talk, to communicate more effectively, because we have to if we want this to function at all. I know a lot of partners of ASD people in vanilla relationships who don't do that. The ASD person goes into their own little world, and the couple has a lot of challenges. They've come to us and asked, "How do you guys have such a good marriage?" Well, we have to talk; the M/s forces us to talk. (And of course there's kinky sex involved, but I don't tell them about that.) It's definitely something that has strengthened our relationship overall, because we have these rituals and protocols in place, because we have structures to lean on, and because we are forced to communicate. It keeps us going in spite of the difficulties of our neurodivergence.

Master Penguin: During and after the title competition, we had a lot of people come up to us and affirm what we suspected. Several were saying, "I have (fill in the blank), and I'm so glad you're up there talking about it, because this is something we deal with too," and then they want to glean information off of us. It became very obvious early on that we'd done the right thing, because there are other people out there with these unseen disabilities who don't feel represented, and they can watch us present and say, "There's one of us up there!" It validates them as being part of the community.

To new people who are in our situation, I'd say first of all that yes, you can absolutely do this kind of relationship. We've proven it, and I've seen many other couples who have also proved that. Second, you should be sure that you understand your diagnosis. Make sure that what you think you have going on is what you actually have. If that means you have to go to a professional and get the diagnosis, by all means do so. Try to understand what it means, What should you expect if you're on the autism spectrum? We hear a lot of misconceptions and rumors about what it's like—find out and make sure. If you're experiencing and living it, you should be able to get a handle on which of these qualities and behaviors are true for you or not. We know that not every symptom is experienced by everybody; for example, autism sometimes manifests differently in women and men. At least get an idea of what you're in for, on both sides.

Once you've got a good grasp on that, you are probably aware of where the challenges and roadblocks are going to be. When those things occur, that's when you can develop structure, protocols, rituals—whatever works—to help ease up those chokepoints. Overall, the best advice I would give is to go slow. Sometimes new folks will look at us and say, "Oh, man, you guys make it look so easy!" They don't understand that we've been working at this for more than twenty years. Every day we adjust, we tweak, we communicate. If this is really what you want, if you're in this for the long haul ... go slow, take it easy, and understand that some days will be successes and some days won't. But as long as you're working towards the same goal together, you can absolutely get there.

Slave ginna: To an s-type with the M-type on the spectrum, I would say, be patient! Don't take the things they say and do personally. Sometimes his moods are just his moods! As a neurodivergent female, I can say that if the M-type is feminine, sensory issues can get worse during certain hormonal times of the month, and you may have to take that into account. As someone who has both been married to and raised folks on the spectrum, it's a little different for each one! You have a base situation with being on the spectrum, but you can talk to fifty ASD folks and they will all manifest it slightly differently. For example, our one son is a more extroverted ASD person, so he really wants those personal connections, but he doesn't always know how to make them effectively. Our other son—who was assigned female at birth but is transitioning—is more of an introverted type, so he really doesn't care if he makes friends with people or what they think of him.

So that has to be taken into consideration. Also, if there are other comorbid conditions, like ADD which sometimes comes with ASD, those will have to be taken into consideration as well. So don't take things personally, and remember to communicate. Lean into your dynamic to make you both successful. If you have an ASD M-type who doesn't initiate conversations, maybe set aside a specific time where you guys can talk. Build it into the schedule.

Something I have to remember for myself is that when I need to get word vomit out and just vent, I have to tell him, "OK, I'm venting,

I don't need you to resolve anything." I have to let him know that up front so that he doesn't get frustrated. So be open and communicate about that sort of thing. Use your dynamic to give you strength.

I'm really glad that discussions about neurodiversity are coming into the M/s community and that it's being talked about more, because if you're going to be fully inclusive, you have to think about disabilities. With us being the kind of subculture we are, we attract quirky people more often than other subcultures, because we may tend to be misfits anyway.

Master Penguin: That was part of the reason we threw it into our platform, because the theme at the conference when we ran was Diversity. And we may discuss a lot of other issues when we bring up Diversity, but we tend to forget about disability and mental health. But we've heard from enough people to know that this is real, people are struggling with it, and they are glad it's finally being discussed and represented. We can only hope this trend continues.

Interview with Toby and girl

Toby: We've been together for more than two decades; girl was a secondary partner during my first marriage. I had to give her up when that was falling apart but once the dust had settled she was there for me. We negotiated a power exchange and a relationship and moved in together. Then we started a family, which meant that a lot of the power exchange had to take a back seat. But I still have authority over most things with her. While I have the final say on a lot of things, I don't throw my weight around. There is a carve-out for her job – I won't interfere with that – and if she should take other partners, which she is free to do, I wouldn't interfere with those relationships.

I accepted that I had Aspergers Syndrome a couple of years ago. She, however, knew about it when we first met all those years ago. She's an early childhood teacher, and works with special ed kids, so she figured it out quickly. I pooh-poohed it for years, but eventually I had to accept it, and I'm learning to see how it affects me.

I like planning and I really like having a routine, but I can be thrown off by disruptions. I can be flexible if I know something is likely to be changed, like projects at my job or travel, but once I've planned my day, if there's a big interruption—like the kid calls home sick and needs to be picked up from school—I can be thrown off. I'll lose focus for the rest of the day and be irritable.

I think I got into power exchange because I love having control. When I have control over a situation, I can reduce the amount of chaos. I don't like chaos in my environment, but unfortunately, I am a source of chaos in my environment—not putting things away, making messes, that sort of thing. Being in control means I have help controlling that.

Girl: The biggest drawback to his ASD is that he can't hold a regular job for a long time. He gets interested in something new and needs to move on and follow the new special interest. On the plus side, though, he's always interesting!

Toby: Do you remember after the 2004 election when George W. Bush talked about having political capital? Well, I have a lot of what I'd call power capital, and I have to be careful where I spend it. I try to be conscious of when I'm using power, so that I don't become a bulldozer and run over other people. That's not easy, because I tend to leak power and overstep my bounds. It's an ongoing struggle.

Girl: I definitely have some ADHD issues in my own neurology, and I can be a little scatterbrained. I grew up as a military brat, and my father was a very demanding and controlling person, so when I grew up and got out on my own, it was very easy for me to fall into that situation again—living with a demanding and controlling person, with rules and structure.

Toby: I spent my childhood with my nose in a book, and then at some point I decided that people were actually interesting and I wanted to interact with them—except they all thought I was an obnoxious asshole. So I had to consciously learn how to read physical cues since it didn't come naturally. This actually makes me good at BDSM, because I can carefully watch the bottom's body and figure out what's going on with them. Outside of BDSM, I'm very good at seeing the flow of power—

Girl interjects: When you are paying attention!

Toby: Yes, when I am paying attention. Or I can be oblivious. When I am paying attention, my focus and intensity can be exciting and make someone feel spotlighted. So those are places where my ASD qualities help the power exchange. Plus there are my general brainy superpowers and all kinds of varied interests that range over time, which gives me an impressive depth of conversation.

Where my ASD gives us problems is around not paying enough attention to people and their needs. Social interaction with anyone is a conscious effort. Saying hello when she comes home is something I'm not good at. Also, I'm very intense and intimidating, sometimes when I don't mean to be. That intensity can cause problems at home and at work. As a child, my parents told me that I was too intense and I didn't understand what they meant.

Girl: I generally know how to un-intensify you and de-escalate the situation, but for other people it can be a problem.

Toby: If I could give advice for new doms who have ASD: First, everybody, ASD or neurotypical, who is in a position of authority should have a therapist. It's easy to find rule lists or procedures for ordinary interaction, like shaking hands or exiting a conversation. I find these very useful. There are many helpful sets of rules that I use to navigate my relationships. I learned about the rules for fighting fair a long time ago, and I lean on those heavily. I know what I need to do in conflict. I have a set of rules I set for myself about how to maintain and nurture intimate relationships. There are all kinds of complex human interactions that it's much easier for me to navigate if I've got a good set of tools for interpersonal conflict and negotiation.

Girl: And they should read all the books, essays, forums, and chat files about how D/s works on a practical level, be actively observant, take notes about what works, and please get a mentor.

Toby: I had a mentor at the beginning, although I didn't call it that. My mentor was just someone we hung out with, someone I could talk to about BDSM, somebody who had far more experience than I did. It doesn't need to be explicit or formal. Second, go out and make friends; it will be uncomfortable, but it's rewarding in a lot of ways. It gets you a social network and a support network, and also gets you references for potential partners.

Third, work on watching people. Get offline and into the real world and hang out with people who are more experienced than you. I don't understand people as well online as I do in real life, because I can't figure out the social cues, so if you have a hard time with that, resort to real-time. Honestly, the people I've encountered in real life had better life skills than the people I encounter online. Also, I learn a lot from hearing about and watching other people's mistakes. If I can hear about their pitfalls, I can make a better plan for the road ahead.

Most importantly: Know yourself and your own weaknesses and limitations, because they'll keep tripping you up. Just admit when you're wrong and learn to fix things and move on.

Girl: If I could give advice to an s-type who is thinking about getting involved with an ASD master type, I'd say that you shouldn't take it all so seriously. You're both just people, and it's easy to get wrapped up in the ideal. Sometimes it can be an opportunity to learn to guide someone else from the bottom. You can teach someone a lot from the bottom, if you can do it respectfully.

Also, appreciate how much fun they are! People with ASD are so colorful and have so much to give—much more than people who don't have the same fractals in their personality.

A Nice Cup of Tea, and Earplugs, Please

Mathom and alvonina

Mathom: I wanted to be on the dominant side of a power dynamic because, as I have told many others, this structure makes the Universe feel right. I have a sense of responsibility, humility, and love when someone submits to me. The further they kneel to me (in flesh or spirit), the more I want to protect them and seek the best for them, so it pulls out the better qualities in me– which didn't seem like a bad thing at all.

When I am alone and unattached, I would say that I am quiet, calm, and very dull because I go about my day with nothing to say to anyone. It is when others are in the mix that the ASD is self-evident. This is partly why it took me so long even to know that I was on the spectrum and how it played poorly with others, because I was single, lived alone, worked nights, and had only myself. I was very contented.

On a daily basis, I would always rather be alone in a quiet area with enough light to see. Most places have "too much" activity in sight and sound. I can take a long while to process events involving other people; that is, the circumstances and what was said need to be sifted through to be absorbed. I may be able to give an immediate response or action, but unless it is a routine one, it will have been incomplete— like this essay. I rarely contemplate my ASD, and only ever attempt to explain it to my servant, so that they can understand me. My emotions are fairly muted and limited, but when I feel them, they are intense and usually overwhelming to others.

I am run more by logical thinking than emotions when assessing a situation or a person. I can only go by what others have described me to be, because I feel I want perfectly normal things, such as my desires for a quiet, solitary area in medium light. A rainy day is pure heaven— gray and the rain covers the sound of the outside, and silences the animals; I have had less experience with snow, but it seems like it would be the most sublime blanket over a calm and muted world.

I am also physically limited, so my servant is my caregiver, on top of domestic service. I haven't pondered a title for it, but valet seems closest, as she helps me bathe and dress, as well as cook, and clean while keeping our calendar of social activities in order.

I rabidly dislike human touch. If it is for a medical examination, or to save my life, I won't like it but fully understand it is necessary. Otherwise, I would rather never be touched because I do not find it comfortable. I am not consoled by touch, and I do not express happiness with a need to hug. I once meditated on the idea of never-ever-ever being touched again, and I swear, I felt pure bliss at the idea. Conversely, and perhaps paradoxically, I am very tactile—I love to touch. I was often scolded as a child for constantly touching by being told, "See with your eyes, not your hands". I am asexual, with no interest in a sexual relationship; albeit the M/s as expressed might be seen as sexual because we are home nudists and I may touch her anywhere, anytime.

I have painfully learned that what consoles and inspires me is not what works for those around me, so I cannot give "words of encouragement" as it will often have the opposite effect. I desire routine, consistency, and clear structures for behavior which also need to be logical. I will naturally balk at and avoid arbitrary rules, particularly if I see benefit in doing the contrary.

I have issues with presumed authority. If one is competent, then by all means lead, but far too many gain a position and then seem compelled to flaunt their ineptitude by being oppressive, unwavering, and—worst of all to me—lacking intelligent consideration. I often wondered if being the eldest child made me comfortable in a leading role, as I was expected to help guide and discipline my siblings, as well as cousins who lived only a few miles away. I always strive for balanced control, led by the memory of the adults around me being more anger-and-aggression-driven; acting before asking questions. I would speak to the family members first to have them consider their words and actions, avoiding anything physical, and even then, give more of a tap of reprimand than anything that would leave a mark. That said, I took my appointed responsibility quite seriously from a young age, so it is difficult to parse a time when I did not have responsibility over others, and did so to the best of my ability, so it only seemed natural that I would take that mantle as an expression of love.

I absolutely know that my ASD wants clear, concise rules, and procedures. I even consider it my love language, as it is something I want to give when I care for someone, if any aspect of their lives needs such. I am quite contented if they no longer require any such boundaries. Honestly, I want them to outgrow some rules.

I would like to think that my ASD allows me to examine situations to find solutions. I will try again and again and again to discover the root cause of a problem. My process can move in very small and precise ways that others would see as leading to the same outcome, but in actuality there is a difference. I seem to notice many details others simply never see, and I hope that makes me able to "read" someone when they aren't able to know they need to speak, or can't at the moment find the words. I can more often be appealed to by a logical debate than an emotional one. I want things the way I want things; on the positive side, it can bring consistency into a situation even if that is "consistent change". I believe that because I have shown myself to be capable, this is why people often feel very comfortable talking to me very openly and seeking advice.

The most difficult part of having ASD in a relationship is helping others understand my differences, which can easily be perceived as being onerous, obnoxious, or come across as assuming entitlement. It affects what I do and how I do it, most especially at a kink club which often has little inclination for any type of accommodation. I believe that the tolerance I am given is more the consequence of my having been a member of the local community for decades, combined with great advocacy and awareness campaigns, so I spend less time explaining the entire concept of ASD and can get to the point regarding my specific needs.

Those needs do cause conflict, most especially when it comes to communication. There are times when I simply cannot grasp what is meant. I know the meanings of the words (most of the time), but cannot fathom how the person is intending me to receive them. This leads to the converse issue where I am trying very hard to make myself be understood, but the other person is simply not grasping it. For both situations, I can never be certain if it is ASD or lack of enough commonality to understand.

I want things the way I want things, which can often inconvenience someone, but my inner calm is disturbed when I have to make a point about it. If my leaving the room fixes the problem, I am more likely to do that than demand that the music and/or lighting be reduced, for example. Then again, there are times—such as in my relationship—when I must address the concern, which can be mentally exhausting on both sides because the need for clarity is intrinsic, so I will push and push until I get there. There must be complete understanding to prevent any future confusion (one hopes). This is probably the toughest aspect in my dynamic, as presumption has only ever brought discord. It can lead to what might be seen as excessive attention, but that is me observing and questioning to ensure that comprehension is achieved. There are few things I dislike more than confusion.

If I could advise someone who wanted to be on the dominant side of a power dynamic—even if they weren't ASD, but especially if they were—I would bring up that communication is the absolute key component of creating a healthy, and thriving dynamic. Being open and honest about thoughts and feelings is crucial. Presuming makes a mess. I have also learned so very much about my ASD from being in a power dynamic, which I infer is the same for any partners—they learn about themselves through the other.

alvonina: First, I had to get used to being corrected every day due to miscommunication, and having to act as a translator when in mixed company. There will be days where I feel that I'm constantly in "trouble" due to communication difficulties where I just can't get my point across, and they can't get me to understand theirs, because our languages are so uniquely different. It will always be my problem, because it is my job to figure out how to translate their communication styles with my own and that of the world around us. I had to learn to just "shut up and do the service", and then we'll figure out where the miscommunication came from afterwards so that the task gets done on a timely basis, and I feel heard.

Due to growing up in the deep south as a child of deeply religious neurotypical parents, I have had the luxury of having to read between the lines for what people are saying versus what they actually mean. My Sir actually means what they say directly, and that is always an unusual thing for those around us who are used to trying to figure out ulterior motives and whatnot. That bluntness is refreshing most of the time, and I find it hilarious when people try to figure out what they mean when it really is just what they said. However, that often leads to frustrations when direct commands aren't obeyed by others, and it took me far too long to try to not read other information into what was said. I admit that I still do it as a habit since I have to do it for every other human in my life.

In some ways I had to become bilingual, in a sense, to both figure out how to speak in a way that they understand, learn what they truly mean, and then take all that together to translate to any other persons involved. Over-asking permission to do things, especially moving anything of theirs (even perceived garbage), is best, since they have built their happy place/nest/retreat and if it is disturbed it wreaks havoc upon their sensibilities. I had to learn how to rephrase (and rephrase again) questions to get the answer that I was looking for, or begin the question with a simple "I'm looking for this type of answer" before you ask. (Oftentimes, however, stating that you want a yes/no-type answer rarely works.)

Tone is a huge thing for my Sir, and I'm quite oblivious to how my tone comes out, so that's still something we're working on after all these years. They are extremely sensitive to outside stimuli and how people interact with them, but all in all they aren't really emotional on any level. Their emotions are anger, joy and sadness, and that's seriously it. Any complex emotions just aren't in their brain to pull from, but the emotions they do have are the most vibrant, pure and extraordinarily explosive and will fill the room when they occur. If I need other emotions from them, I will take the time to ask if we can talk and then afterwards ask to talk to other people about whatever I need to discuss and between us and my Sir we usually figure out what's going on.

I had to learn that many things they do were perceived as "backwards" by me, the neurotypical partner, and I had to adjust to living in that world which wasn't my own. After I got over the initial shock, which I admit took me far too many years, seeing my Sir be in their utter-glee-zero-fucks-given moments does bring a smile to my face. There's this preconceived notion of how an adult should act, and singing/dancing in public spaces is not on that list; neither is talking to oneself or touching nearly everything that you pass by.

Patience is a virtue, and I had to learn to not beat myself up for my learning process of existing in an ASD person's space. The nesting habits of my Aspergers Top Letter drive me utterly batty, for all I see is clutter and mess, while it is their happy place. They know where everything is, but I only see a crazy amount of disorganization, and this is one of the things that makes me less likely to want others to see our home. I try to pride myself on being put together, having a kept home and an organized workspace, but I feel like a failure when I walk into the communal area and see "the Nest". Those who are closest to us don't even notice the clutter as being a mess like I do, so I'm aware that the issues of perspective are fully mine.

I have to be prepared to bring several bags everywhere we go, for entertainment, comfort, and sensory situations. I also had to get used to being the "adult" when it comes to dealing with figures of authority, government paperwork, and other important documentation. I often find myself at a crossroads of trying to caretake rather than caregive, since my Sir also has physical ailments, and I myself have a triggery past with being the caretaker of my less-than-pleasant mother, so we've had to deal with that baggage over the years as well. At times it feels like I am parenting my Sir because of all the things that I have to bring any time we leave the home. Between my toy bag/s and their sensory bags, I'm then playing the role of pack pony in a less than sexy way, though they do enjoy watching the struggle of me being stubborn in getting everything moved from place to place in one go.

Having to be the anchor while in social situations is honestly my primary service to them. I'm their safe space, their home base, and the person who will make damned sure that they are left alone and that their time in public is as comfortable as possible. Being away from the home requires taking many of the "Nest"s' happy-place items with us. We have to pack, and remember to take, a collection of sensory items, medications, crafting items, books and other random tiddly bits that serve a means of comfort in an otherwise stressful situation. Ear plugs are a requirement anywhere we go at a minimum, and there must be a way that they can keep their phone charged, so plugs and/or battery packs are in the bag.

Sensory differences apply to every aspect of day-to-day life as an overwhelming experience. This includes chiding the neighbors upstairs for their smoking choices, needing both hot and cold beverages at mealtime, textural issues in clothing options, ear plugs being needed pretty much everywhere to dull the pitch and tones of noise, and having sunglasses and hats (or avoiding crazy weather in general). Being in the deep south, we are often riddled with magma-like weather, and my Sir is highly susceptible to the heat waves, so sometimes it is just easier for them to stay inside and be an introverted hermit and I will go to the event myself.

In our vanilla lives we do work together, and I'm actually the boss of my Sir, which of course makes everything interesting; but mainly it is another way to see how their Aspie brain works in stressful situations. They are easily distracted if I give more than one task at a time, and when I do have to do that, I have to give it to them in a certain order with notes so that things will get done in an efficient way for us both.

Our M/s is a purely non-sexual service-based relationship (Master of the House/valet, maid/majordomo/etc.) so we already are the odd people out in the kink groups. It's hard sometimes, needing physical play or sexual touch and not being able to get it from my Sir, but we've found that my needs can be met outside of the relationship (with permission of course) by others.

If you are an s-type contemplating a power dynamic with an ASD Top Letter, be aware that mixing kink or power exchanges into this should be gradual. That way, you can learn the other person's "isms" and how they function in day-to-day life, so that when it is vital to communicate in a clear and concise manner, you're able to do that even when in a kink situation.

They are often a fount of specific information, and you might not find any wiggle room with rules, or that you have to lay down extremely specific sets of boundaries. They are terribly creative and will have their head in the clouds, rather than being down to earth with mundane conversations. Go slow; it's worth the frustration of learning now to "not people" around an ASD person.

The joy that I get from serving someone who is as eclectic as my Sir is immense even as it is frustrating. I take it as a challenge, something that I can strive to do better throughout the years, and at the same time not only make their lives better as they have made mine, but continue to maintain peaceful and comfortable living situations for us both. I also enjoy the sly moments of service out in public that are just seen as me helping them and not being anything kinky while, for us, it sure as hell is kinky even when I serve them a nice cup of tea.

Interview with A and Jay

A: We've been together in some capacity for about five months, so at this point we're still working on the beginning building blocks. As should probably be the case for any relationship, we haven't just jumped into the power dynamic fully from the get-go. We're still experimenting together, and seeing where it goes. For example, today we were talking about different rituals we might like to try out. We're going to start with a small morning and nightly ritual, which has been really nice to figure out, and hopefully will be nice to do as well.

Jay: We're slowly easing ourselves into it. Sort of a D/s sample platter so far. Very lovely. It's my first time trying any of this very seriously, and it's been quite enjoyable. I'm very subservient in the bedroom; I'm not afraid to ask for things, but I still serve. Outside the bedroom, we're still figuring out the areas of authority—what I wear when we go out, where we go out to. We're still exploring having A be the controlling party. That's been very pleasant as well.

A: I'm constantly in the process of learning how my neurology affects me; at the moment I notice it most in interpersonal interactions, as well as the sensory issues that crop up for me. I am very literal-minded, and I will often miss the more subtle kind of not being serious. I'm pretty good at catching obvious jokes, but when things aren't 100% spelled out, I can miss the underlying double meaning or come to the wrong conclusion about it. I tend to be very open and literal and honest in my communication.

My senses get overwhelmed easily, especially with bright lights, sudden or loud noises, and strong scents. Tastes I'm mostly okay with; I don't have a lot of food sensitivities, fortunately. But I'm paradoxically also very sensory-seeking a lot of the time; I love deep pressure and strong flavors, and often listen to my music fairly loud, because it's a predictable and consistently enjoyable kind of stimulus. Music is a big thing for my brain, and I listen to it in a way that feels very uniquely autistic and joyful to me. I'll find a song that resonates with me and just listen to it on repeat over and over again, until I find another one that scratches that same itch in my brain, and then move on to that one. The repetition helps me really dive deep and wring out every ounce of nuance and pleasure from it, but I recognize that most people don't have the capacity to fixate on a single song like that and still derive enjoyment from the experience.

I very much rely on routines on a daily basis; I'd define a routine as specifically *how* I do something, which I stick to pretty rigidly, whereas *when* I do something is a bit easier for me to be flexible with. For example, I have routines for catching the bus, brushing my teeth, getting into bed, packing my bag when I go out, and so on, and it's important to me that I do those things in the same way each time.

Another pretty big thing for me is having trouble with eye contact; it's intense enough that it actually activates my fight or flight response if I do it for too long. It almost feels like staring into the sun, that feeling of absolute overwhelm and so completely needing to look away with every fiber of my being. When I'm in a conversation I'll just look over somewhere else—in fact, I'm doing it right now! I also have difficulty modulating my tone of voice, so when I get enthusiastic or excited about something, my voice will just raise in volume, so in those moments I have to be very conscious about how I actually come across when I'm speaking.

Jay: I definitely notice their issues with volume, which can make it interesting when you have flatmates, but it's still very endearing. They also have a very unusual taste in music; it's awesome to listen to all the different pieces of music they find, many of which are very strong in emotion and evoke a certain kind of passion, in some sense. I think it may be indicative of them wanting to re-experience that emotion a whole bunch, and then—OK, now let's find a different one!

A: Everything in my life is bound up with me experiencing the world in this incredibly intense and concentrated way, and my inclination towards a D/s dynamic is no exception. For one thing, I love the emphasis on clear communication, being able to state what you want and what you're looking for. I don't have to endlessly keep guessing, or try and figure out the whole neurotypical flirting thing. I'll never be able to do the steps to the "Do they or don't they?" dance, but here everything is very clear, very ritualized, very methodical. It's easy, and moreover *expected*, to have discussions about what you mean when you say something, or what you want. The "no until yes" framework around consent that's so foundational to BDSM means that I don't have to constantly be wary of surprises, and I don't have to guess what behaviors are expected of me because either they've been discussed and I know what to do or they haven't and I know incorporating them isn't something I need to worry about.

In addition, the very deliberate nature of what a BDSM scene looks like helps me be fully in the moment. There's something that starts it and something to accomplish in the middle, and then something that means it's concluded. I enjoy myself more because I don't have to worry about the uncertainty of what I'm supposed to be doing, whether we're done or if there's more. It's all very structured in my head and I always have that structure to fall back on, and that's really nice.

Speaking of structure, my need for routine carries over into my experience with kink as well. Whenever I engage in a scene, my routine consists of first going through a mental checklist for setup. I make sure I have everything necessary for cleanup and aftercare, lube, a place where all my tools are organized in the way I'm expecting, a tidy play area, a radius of clear space around where I and any associated parties will be, and lastly I check if there's anything new that could interfere or that I'm not expecting. In that same way, part of working with rope for me just intrinsically means keeping my shears with my rope, and then in an easily accessible and safe spot when I start tying. I also check in every time I finish a section of a tie, to make sure that it feels okay and hasn't shifted the tension or feeling of the rest of it. That might all sound like a lot to remember, but the point is that I don't have to think about or consciously remember every step because I make sure to take care of it all in the same way each time, and that frees up my brain for thinking about the rest of the scene.

I will say that there are moments when I have to deal with things that probably wouldn't bother someone who isn't autistic. I've been in the middle of a scene and needed to stop for a minute because I could feel the seam of my sock cutting into my toes, and I had to fix that before I could continue. And something that comes up periodically is that in the same way that eye contact is overstimulating, sometimes just being visually perceived can be equally as painful. In settings of heightened sensitivity and intimacy I become a lot more aware of my body, of how I'm existing in the space, and what's going on in terms of sensations, and so things that are usually okay can become way too intense. I've had times where I'm really feeling it, but I can't handle being visually perceived, so I've gone, "Okay, I need you to not be looking at me right now, so I'm going to blindfold you." And that works because I *am* the one in charge and I have the flexibility to cater to my own needs, so on the whole even with those challenges I don't think my being autistic negatively impacts our dynamic.

Jay: I agree! I find it adorable.

A: I find that being autistic does actually help in some ways, first and foremost because the world of kink and BDSM is one of my ongoing special interests. I really love learning everything I can and being able to get actively involved, and that adds another layer of appreciation outside of just thinking it's cool. Being in this world is so actively enriching to me in a way that I think not a lot of kinky people get to experience. And when I'm interacting with Jay, it means that I can get into a very focused headspace where I don't have to worry about outside concerns or anything else that might be bothering me. All of my brain is focused solely on what I'm doing, whether that's impact play, or the words I'm saying, or some sensation I'm chasing.

Jay: I would agree that it's pretty great to be someone's special interest.

A: Kink being one of my special interests actually really helps me to be a responsible dom. It's much easier for me to learn and incorporate information if I understand why, so the fact that I can really delve into whatever I want to learn and connect it to all the other information I know means that I can retain a lot of knowledge around what to look out for. It's like there's this bank of information in my head that I can pull from whenever I need to, either to actually apply when I'm in a scene or just share verbally. A decent amount of the dirty talk that I do also lives in that bank of information, so I don't have to worry about actively coming up with each individual phrase or tripping over my words (which is something I do frequently!) because I have so many already figured out and scripted and I can just toss them out whenever I need to. And as a corollary to that, I'm a lot more deliberate with the things I *do* say unscripted, and I'll often rehearse them in my mind once or twice before speaking them out loud.

Jay: It's very hot!

A: Something I've realized as I've started exploring a more formal D/s dynamic is that sex is inherently kinky for me; I don't think I have ever in my life genuinely enjoyed or desired anything vanilla. This is partially due to being nonbinary and on the ace and stone spectrums, but my autism in addition to that particular combination of things makes a D/s dynamic incredibly fulfilling for me, and as I explore more with Jay I'm learning that I truly need it in a relationship. I should also clarify that when I say kinky I don't mean inherently rough or aggressive; I can be astonishingly tender and soft and loving, and I often am! But there's some form of power dynamic in play at all times. There's this unspoken undercurrent of "I'm letting you do this because I want you to, and if I didn't then you wouldn't be doing it" even more than what just baseline consent calls for, and as someone who needs things to be a very particular way a lot of the time I find a lot of comfort in knowing that dynamic is there and cherished at all times.

Jay: My advice to someone thinking about being in my position? Subtlety is for suckers. Be clear and forthright and honest, maybe even to the point of what other people would consider too much information. Leave as many areas as black and white and not gray as you can. This will make you feel more comfortable when they are intensely present and focused on something that you're enjoying, so if you're not enjoying it you can say so right away, and it won't be blindsiding to them. Also, it's a lot easier for them to understand as well. It will be more successful for both of you.

A: What I would say to dominants on the spectrum: never back down from the chance to be clear about what you need, who you are, and what you bring to the relationship. I draw tremendous power from knowing that not only am I encouraged to articulate my needs and work to have them fulfilled, but it's actively expected that I'll be in charge and communicate exactly what I want. Don't be afraid to share that side of yourself with your submissive. I usually don't know how I feel about a new thing in the moment, and need time (sometimes up to a few days) to process and figure it out, but I'm very open about when I'm not feeling comfortable or certain of something and it's only ever strengthened how I fit within the dynamic. Know that there will *always* be a place for you here, you with all your needs and desires and quirks that the world says are atypical, and there is such joy and fulfillment waiting for you along this path.

Interview with Dr. Bob Rubel and constants

Dr. Bob Rubel: Well, right off, I want to thank you, Raven, for this second interview, many years after the one in *Broken Toys*. I'm a great fan of yours. You have added vast knowledge to many fascinating areas of gender identity, spirituality, and relationships. Thanks, also, to Joshua who doubtless must go through all these interviews and sanitize them to some extent before you take them on. Lots of work. Thank you for that.

So, you've asked me to bring the story current from the prior interview. Wow! I'm not sure how much detail you want, but you can always edit this down. (Inhales deeply...)

The structure of my current relationship differs from previous relationships. The last time you interviewed me, I had a different Master. That partner had come into my life from the swingers' community without any background in BDSM, let alone experience in authority-imbalanced dynamics. Once I began bringing her to M/s conferences, she realized she wanted ours to be an M/s relationship. That journey is a tale unto itself.

At any rate, after about four years together (2014) when I was again writing M/s books, we were taking personality tests and values clarification exercises and so forth to learn more about ourselves and each other. It was at this point we discovered that a few of our values differed enough that we were pretty sure they were irreconcilable. (It was as if one person liked to vacation in the mountains and the other preferred to go to the ocean. One wasn't better than the other, but they weren't compatible if you are looking for a stress-free vacation together.) Working through these tests and quizzes definitely helped us to understand why we were having so much friction in our relationship. After 7½ years, we concluded it was a good time to "close" our relationship. This was in 2017.

This story is about the transition point to my current life. That dissolution occurred the weekend before she and I were scheduled to run a High Protocol Leather Dinner for our local MAsT Chapter. We had spent about eight contact hours training the MAsT Chapter slave-servers, and had developed an entire curriculum. Furthermore, I was to serve as the majordomo at the dinner itself. Suddenly she didn't want to appear at an M/s meeting with me, as she didn't want to give our community the impression that we were still together.

Well, there was only one other person in this city who knew High Leather Protocol dining, and that was The Goddess Indigo. The local MAsT Chapter president asked if I'd be willing to serve Goddess Indigo, as Jen was not coming. I believe I said something to the effect of: "Is the Pope Catholic?" The Goddess Indigo and I had initially met in about 2004 and we had been in the same MAsT Chapter since about 2005. Also, I'd used her as my real estate agent a few times, so we knew one another, even if casually.

So, at this point, I'm in New Orleans at DomCon and the Leather Dinner is the next Friday. On Monday, once I was home, I called Goddess Indigo and asked whether it would be convenient to meet on Wednesday—two days away. I needed to know of any private protocols I should be aware of. The answer was "No." The meal went off without a hitch. The Goddess was at the head table (technically, she outranked the host) and I stood off her right shoulder directing the serving slaves.

In the days and weeks after that dinner, she and I started exploring the idea that maybe we could actually become a couple. It was improbable—we were different in many ways—but our core values were the same and our breadth of M/s knowledge seemed similar; she, too, was a national conference presenter with stature. So we began having dinners together and spoke often on the phone. After about six months, while she was at a conference without me, she called and apologized for having to say this over the phone, but, "This isn't going to work."

I asked, "Why would that be, Master?"

She said, "Well, with your last Master, you had a sex partner, a play partner for whom you were the Top, an assistant to help sell your books at conferences, and so forth. I'm just not all those things."

"What do you want to do about that, Master?" I asked.

"I think you should go out and find someone else," she said. "You need someone to touch your romantic side. You need a sex partner, because you and I are not that." (We'd agreed within the first few weeks that sexual entanglement would contaminate the purity of writing and presenting together.)

So I started to explore dating sites. I blew up three credit cards as I fell for dating sites that were scams. None of those paths let me to anyone who would meet in real life. I went back to looking through Fetlife ads for *women seeking men.*

By pure chance, on April 21 I was working in my computer while being driving back to Austin from Oklahoma LeatherFest by my former slave, and I happened to check that group on Fetlife. Wow, there was a new post. A woman had posted an ad the prior day that sounded very interesting. I sent her a private message that I'd seen her post and that I'd be interested in meeting her. She was actually online at the time, so we typed back and forth for about ten minutes and agreed to have a drink the next evening — Monday, April 22.

That person turned out to be my lifemate; a magical fit. We've been together ever since.

constants: Within a few hours of posting my ad, I had six men asking if they could meet me. I was floored. I'd been out of the local scene for a bit over seven years. I had two very-grown children. Six men within a few hours! I couldn't make any sense of it. Then Dr. Bob's note came in, roughly 24 hours after my post. I looked him up after our Fetlife exchanges and then Googled him. I stayed up all night reading every single thing I could find about him. There were massive amounts of information, including his own Wikipedia page!

We agreed to meet the next evening at 6pm at a nice restaurant/bar we both knew. Slightly late, I hurried into the bar. I recognized him from having seen him do a fire presentation at a meeting years before, when I had been more active in the community. He got up as I approached his table. He turned to me with a big smile on his face and asked: "May I hug you?"

OMG!

We sat down and ordered water. We hit it off instantly. Time went by and he deftly answered my barrage of questions. The waitress kept stopping to ask us if we wanted to order anything, and we kept saying, "Thank you, but not quite yet." After about 40 minutes of this, he asked about ordering dinner. I replied, "No, thank you."

Well … that put him in an awkward place. We were taking up a booth in an upscale restaurant and it was dinnertime. If we weren't going to eat here, then…? He turned to me and asked: "Would you like to come to my apartment? I live about 20 minutes from here."

I replied, "Yes, please." I don't think he was expecting to bring me home. He's a "by-the-book" kind of guy and "taking an unknown woman to your house 40 minutes after meeting her" was not on his list of "OK behaviors". At any rate, he put a $20 bill on the table for the wait staff and off we went!

Again, as an indication of his mental attitude, it didn't dawn on him that I might stay the night: I left my car and phone in the parking lot; after all, he was going to bring me back, later.

This was the moment my life changed completely.

Dr. Bob Rubel: I'd already told Master (The Goddess Indigo) about this meeting—she was well aware of what was going on—and all she said was, "That's fine, boy. Call me when she leaves."

The next morning around 11, Master called and said semi-jokingly, "Boy! You were supposed to call me after she left!" As the girl was only a few feet from me, I tried to whisper into the phone: "Master, she hasn't left!" Master laughed and laughed and said, "Call me and fill me in on this once you have the opportunity." By mid-afternoon I called and told her that we'd picked up her car, but she was still here with me.

And constants never left. That's why she carries that name: she is a "constant" in my life. We also use that name to get by in Vanillaville. Everyone assumes her name is *Constance*; it isn't.

She stayed at my apartment from the outset because she had just bought a duplex that was being renovated. She had been sleeping at her mother's house. It wasn't so pleasant because it had been vacant for some time. So you might say the choice was an easy one for her. Bottom line: I had found the girl who would enable Master and me to continue *our* relationship.

constants: I got into the lifestyle because I was a leader in my job. I ran my own business. In my private life I just wanted to be able to come home and *not* have to make decisions. I was mentally exhausted by the end of a workday, and I needed to be in a space where I was relieved of that responsibility. I needed a place that would bring me peace of mind.

Previously, I had a Master for a year, but it was never 24/7. He moved away and we ended it. Then I met another Master, and we were together for four years. Similarly, not 24/7 either. He was very involved in the community, so I got to know more about the lifestyle. When that ended, my son was at an age where he wasn't dealing well with me having anyone significant in my life. I decided to stop dating. I waited until my youngest child had finished high school and then I went back on line. I had been away from the community for seven years. It that context, I met Dr. Bob about 24 hours of posting my Fetlife ad. Pretty amazing.

Dr. Bob Rubel: There was quite an adjustment for constants when we began living together, as I'd been living for the previous 17 years in a high protocol M/s. I certainly expected that was going to continue. I had lived in structured dynamics with my first owner (who gave me a slave), and with my immediately-prior Master. I was comfortable living this way and had no reason to expect to change. In fact, most of my early books were about this living style. (My then-publisher called the books, "Live with Dr. Bob and mindi".)

However, as much as I'd expected (wanted) to live in High Protocol with constants, it turned out there was a little twist awaiting me. About three months after we first met, as we were moving into the duplex constants was renovating, a former Leather Brother of mine commented that she was a "little." While I'd seen littles and little competitions at conferences, I'd never explored that subculture.

"What's that supposed to mean?" I asked him.

"It means her core being is that of a much younger person, and you're going to have trouble imposing an M/s dynamic on her."

Well, truer words were never spoken. Without going into details, we set up our structure as "DaddyDom/babygirl" within a High Protocol M/s framework.

As an aside, I'd never in my life been even slightly interested in Daddy/girl structures and didn't view myself as having the "Daddy" kind of nurturing personality. Because of my autism, I never really learned how to be casually social either with men or women. I don't go to parties and avoid group settings.

As time went on, I learned that her little was about 5 or 6. When she was not in "little headspace," the question was: How would we interact? Well, since she is not normally in little headspace, we interact in the formal M/s structure I've always used, even if slightly softened. For example, if I am driving home and she is at home, I will text her when I'm 5 minutes away. She will be waiting for me in a full present position, with the door slightly ajar so I can just nudge it open in case I'm carrying things. She's on the ground in front of me in full Present. So she and I continue to live the same formal lifestyle that I prefer.

I use our evenings (about 6:30-10:30) as bonding times. No television. No phones. No computer work—unless we discussed it during the day and I agreed with it. Our dining room table is always set with china, stemware and silver flatware. We dine nightly in what's called "semi-formal."

(I should make a distinction here: How you are dressed depends on the formality of the event. How you are dressed is separate from what the level of service is called. *Informal* means you are serving 1-3 courses. *Semi-formal* is three to five courses. *Formal* means five or more courses.)

So we dress up in the evenings. Sometimes it's roleplay, sometimes it's adults speaking about adult topics: history, sociology, words. If I have a specific preference the evening, I will tell her the theme and the clothing I wish her to wear. If I don't have a strong opinion, we have a protocol for that.

I have developed a way for her to signal who she wants to be for the evening. On a typical day, we work independently until about six or six-thirty. We have a brief discussion about the direction of the evening. Then shower and change clothes (*changing clothing* is part of the *state change* I need so the fantasy evenings are separated from the workday). We play with our outfits. They range from formal tuxedo or tails to some outrageous outfit or another.

Once I'm dressed, I set up the living room lighting, sound, and visuals. I like the living areas of the house to have dimmed lights (about 3,200-degrees Kelvin), I have a computer connected to a 35" monitor that sits on top of one of the two pianos, opposite the couch. From YouTube, I play a crackling fire or thunderous rain, etc. We have a 55" monitor that plays "movies" I've put together from my own photography. There are (battery-operated) candles around the living room and, weather permitting, a fire in the fireplace.

With this setting completed, I sit on the couch, have my evening cocktail (prepared by Babygirl) and read a book.

(My favorite book at the moment, which I will highly recommend to everyone, is called *Being Wrong: Adventures in the Margins of Error*. It is a fascinating read, and it exposes me to my own stupidity as well as to many of my badly flawed assumptions.)

Once she's dressed (the drink has been pre-made and set out) she enters and presents herself. I say something such as, "Oh wow! The baby is ready to join me!" She comes and kneels before me. I ask, "Whom have I here?" Now, this is an important point. This is when babygirl signals her state of mind. She has to decide how she is going to answer the question. Most commonly, she says, "This is your babygirl, Daddy." In that case, my reply is: "Babygirl! What a delight. You look wonderful! I see you've brought something—what is it?" She answers, "I've brought my neck-uh-lace." (This is her babygirl pronunciation for "necklace", which refers to her collar.)

"Your necklace?" I say. Then, "Why are you bringing it to me?" She then says; "So you can put it around my neck so I can't run away," or something to that effect. I put the collar on her, and then she looks at me as if I should remember something or other. So I wait a bit and then say, "You may continue." She rises, curtsies, walks three paces back, turns and goes to the kitchen to prepare dinner.

On the rare occasions that babygirl becomes a little too informal, I ask her, "How would that sound in protocol?" We are a high-protocol family—I expect her to be walking slightly behind me and to my right when we are in public; I expect her to open doors for me. Once I've had a bite of food, she waits for me to put another bite on my fork and feed it to her before she begins to eat. I expect my bed to be turned down before I get into it. I have lately stepped in to help wash dishes, as this enables her to join me in the living room faster than if I let her do the dishes alone.

Living with a babygirl has forced me to change the way I speak with her, and as a result, speak with almost everybody. I am most cautious about speaking sternly or bringing into our "bubble" anything that is currently on the news. Babygirls can pout if their feelings are hurt, and the last thing I want is a pouty babygirl. So I am much more careful in how I speak. I am much more circumspect about what I say — particularly when she is relaxed and drops into the speech pattern of a five-or-six-year-old. When she regresses too much, I have trouble understanding her. At that point, I ask her to come up just a little bit in age. Living with The Baby has been a growth experience for me, and I appreciate it a tremendous amount.

I know that Master's interview comes at a different point in this book, but I'd add now, that being slave to The Goddess Indigo has been a remarkable experience and has calmed my inner core to a dramatic degree. She is extremely helpful in all ways of my life. She is a very sophisticated NLP Master Practitioner, a certified hypnotherapist, an ordained minister, and a master trainer (specifically, training real estate sales agents). I've learned a great deal from Master; she is very good at managing me. And I am very willing to be managed by her. Master most impresses me because she is so incredibly competent in everything she does.

constants: I'm happier than I've ever been in any relationship. He is the love of my life. I was already a very organized person, fortunately. The protocols are his kink, and I think they also bring him peace of mind. Before I met him, I had an illness that affected by thinking processes, so sometimes I forget things, and he's extremely patient with me when that happens. He introduced the protocols bit by bit—particularly our formal dining protocols. For example, when we first were together, I didn't really care which fork I picked up at dinner;

if it held food I was fine with it. In the early days together, he would say such things as, "babygirl, please use your salad fork," or "You've set the table with white wine glasses and we're serving red wine." He taught me and slowly and gradually introduced the rules of formal dining. It took months. Had he suddenly required me to study the incredibly long list of everything you have to know and do, I think I would have run and hidden under the covers.

He trains in a piecemeal fashion; a little now, a little next week. That way, I could fully absorb a few at a time and master those. Soon there would be the next set. First it would be how he wanted the lights set, and then it would be how he wanted the music set, and then how he wanted the fire burning. I also like things organized, although I am not nearly as extreme as he is. I recognize that I think better when I'm in a clean workspace where my desk is organized and things are laid out and my house is clean. So, I see the value in the way he requires an orderly house. He just does all these things to the nth degree! I try very hard to provide an environment for him which is very stable and free from distractions.

His need for order is the Autism Spectrum Disorder trait I most notice. Another trait is that he doesn't like last-minute changes or surprises, especially if it involves anyone else—my family, or friends, or anyone other than the two of us. He needs advance notice, because it throws him if things aren't the way he expected them to come together. This can be tricky at times, because life doesn't always give you advance warning, and things come up at the last minute. Typical for those on the Spectrum, he needs the events in his life to be set, so he knows what's going to happen, and when and how it's going to happen.

Dr. Bob Rubel: Fortunately, babygirl comes from the legal profession and is as detail-oriented as I am. We have different sets of tools, but right off the bat our problem-solving skills and verbal skill levels were compatible. She is my ideal partner. At the same time, we're very different in personality, and she keeps me much *lighter* than I've ever been in my life.

constants: As a little, I have a very childlike appreciation to life, and I see joy in things from a child's perspective. I think that I bring that out in him and enable him to relax. He's not so on-edge as he was in the beginning. I'm playful and optimistic; I laugh a lot. He likes to hear me laugh. It's all good.

Dr. Bob Rubel: I didn't even know about my ASD until 2006, when my then-owner (Mistress) observed me interacting with my then-slave. There had been a little "upset" between my slave and I and Mistress was in the room. Without going into details, she informed me for the first time that I had Asperger Syndrome. She sent me upstairs to my office where I looked it up.

Upon returning to her, I said. "OK, so I scored 80-90% on the self-test. What am I supposed to do about that?" She told me to start reading about the condition. Hence, my first advice to people with ASD who are getting into this lifestyle is to start reading about it.

My current Master (The Goddess Indigo) and I are enthusiastic about taking self-assessment tests to determine such things as the words/actions you have to hear to feel you've been apologized to; your attachment style, and your personal strengths and weaknesses. We're constantly trying to better understand ourselves, as most of us are blind to who we really are.

Referring back to the book I'm currently reading (*Being Wrong* by Kathryn Schulz), Schultz points out that your own beliefs are really a belief in someone else's belief. The problem is, the person's belief upon which you based *your* belief is itself based on somebody else's belief which is *also* unfounded. Since almost all that one knows is deductively derived, and since the assumptions underlying guess are only probabilities, the fact is that you and I don't know a whole lot about our own environments or our own behaviors that is verifiably accurate.

This has had a big impact on my certainty; it's made me much more humble and forgiving. I'm now working on being comfortable with being uncertain; I'm also much more grateful, in a general way. I am often absolutely certain about things, yet blind to the possibility that my certainty may simply be wrong. The trick is to learn to disentangle one's certainty in order to examine it.

constants: I took the "strengths test," and the test revealed my strengths to be *empathy* and *communication*. One of the skills I bring to the table is the ability to help him formulate and phrase things. This is valuable when he engages in a sensitive topic with someone. He is so honest and so blunt it can be off-putting; it sometimes prevents dialogue. He sometimes starts off with a statement that closes (rather than opens) the door to communication. I help him to see how his wording might be perceived by others. I then rephrase his proposed line so that it conveys the same message—but in a manner that will be better received. This is part of what I bring to our relationship.

This will sound odd from someone who is an empathetic feeling-type, but I think my legal training really helps with this relationship. An attorney's role is to remove emotion from the conflict in order to facilitate discussions that direct both parties toward resolution. Often, clients are having an emotional reaction to the "what happened" part of the case. Frequently, it's the client's emotions which slow or completely prevent a resolution. Lawyers try to step outside of that and develop a more logical approach.

I don't like conflict, and I'm a peacemaker, but when he gets frustrated or short with me, I try hard not to immediately assume that it's something I did (or go to the extreme position that he must not love me anymore). I step back and look at it logically to figure out the cause of his stress. There's always a reason for it. And it may be me—but it seldom is. I have to back out of the emotional part of an upset and not take his behavior personally. Another strategy I use is to mentally eliminate everything else that I sense is going on in his head in order to lead him in the direction of the most likely issue that triggered him.

And then, of course, I can be sensitive about his needs for order and planning so surprises don't throw him for a loop.

Dr. Bob Rubel: I don't mind if she says, "Daddy, may I have permission to go X place at Y time?" The answer is, "Of course." A problem arises when she informs me that she *has* to go someplace *right now*. Is the Babygirl *telling* Daddy that she is willfully going somewhere

I didn't already know about? I realize that sometimes she has to make a decision about a future event when her friends are around and I'm not there. I don't like surprises, and I often become reactive to them. I do realize this is a personal weakness.

Were I making a list of ideal traits in a partner, a "consulting attorney" would be very high on that list. It happens to matter to me that she has been through law school; that's not at all trivial. I said that to her in the beginning. Her legal training translated to me as, "able to adapt to my life." So, for me, this is a relationship made in heaven.

constants: If you're not already a lawyer, I wouldn't suggest someone go to law school as a way to understand their ASD Master. I think it's just a matter of recognizing your Master's needs and not judging them. Figure out areas that create peace of mind for them. Understand what stresses them and conduct yourself accordingly. When things get rocky and tension is building up, step back from the emotion. I very rarely lose my temper—maybe two or three times in five years. Also, I can't go to bed angry; I don't like conflict. I try to look at the big picture, and not to immediately go into self-doubt. Look at what your Master is dealing with. It's fine to ask, "Have I done something to upset you?" However, if the answer is "No,", then I have to accept that. If I see him getting stressed, I'll try to talk to him and figure out what's going on, and maybe nip it in the bud before it explodes.

If nothing else, he doesn't hide it! If he's upset, he'll tell me what he's upset about. That honesty is very reassuring. He'll tell me straight out. If I am asking what's wrong, usually it's because I've got something in my mind that I think he's upset about, and usually I'm wrong. When that happens, I can't decide whether he's lying, or that I'm somehow creating all this and making it worse. If he knows what it is, he will tell me. Of course, sometimes he doesn't exactly know what's upsetting him — he simply can't identify it.

Dr. Bob Rubel: I am very quick to tell her when something is concerning me about her behavior. I don't hold onto that at all. I will bring it up at the first possible opportunity. However, sometimes I'm upset about something else, and it's rubbing off on my behavior. It doesn't have anything whatsoever to do with her, but I'm certainly not in a good mood.

constants: He lives in a world governed by protocols; typical of those on the Autism Scale. I don't think anyone can get them all right, all the time. I certainly can't. Slip-ups happen. But for the most part, he's very good at correcting me in a way that is fun. For example, he may ask: "Is babygirl now telling Daddy what is going to happen next?" His use of humor keeps me from going into a funk thinking I've let him down, or I didn't do something right, or I forgot something. I think that if he didn't have that sense of humor, I would have a really hard time. But he allows for the fact that mistakes happen, and that's OK so long as I didn't do it on purpose. As he teaches, in an authority-imbalanced dynamic everyone involved has to be *willing*.

Dr. Bob Rubel: Initially, I wrote *Protocol Handbook for the Leather slave* to give my former slave a written document about how to live with me. She was no slouch, either; she's an RN paralegal who is very smart. However, she was having trouble keeping the protocols straight, so I wrote it all out at my then-Mistress's order.

The triggering incident for writing the Protocols book happened at South Plains Leatherfest in about 2005. We had gone from our rooms to the elevators on the second floor. We were standing in front of the elevator doors. I assumed my slave was going to press the "down" button; my slave assumed I was going to press the button. My Mistress assumed I was going to press the down button. After about fifteen seconds of immobility, Mistress stepped forward and pressed it. When the elevator doors opened, I assumed that my slave was going to go forward and hold the door open. My Mistress started to move at the same time I did, and the three of us collided. Mistress became extremely angry and told me, "You have six months to teach that woman proper protocols!" And that was how it happened that I wrote the *Protocols* book.

constants: The first time we met, he explained his relationship with The Goddess Indigo, his current Master (not to be confused with his Mistress from 2002-2010). I fell in love with him the night I met him. I was attracted to him by everything I'd read about him. Then I met him, and it was like magic. I've already related our restaurant/bar meeting. Now I'll describe my reaction to the first ten minutes with him at his apartment.

We reached his door on the second floor of an upscale apartment complex about 50 minutes from the center of Austin. I was immediately struck by how clean and neat everything was (he lives this way to this day). There would seldom be anything out of place that couldn't be corrected within five minutes.

He opened the apartment door, walked past the entry to the second bathroom and bedroom and took a slight hook right. That's when you see lots of things, suddenly. A wall filled with woodturnings on their own mounts, the sliding-glass door to the deck crammed with plants and flowers, the entry to the second bedroom and then… then…

And then I saw his six-foot rabbit next to the piano! Dressed in tails with grey lapels; it's on roller skates. He introduced me to Harvey. I was in shock. Harvey … as in "Harvey the invisible pooka" in the movie with Jimmy Stewart! As I was trying to absorb what I was seeing, he sat down at the piano and started playing for me! I was a goner, totally lost.

In the back of my mind, though, I knew I had to pass this test. His Master had to approve me or we couldn't have a relationship. But later I met her and she was absolutely beautiful.

So other than that initial fear that I wouldn't pass the test, it's been wonderful. I feel that our three-way dynamic has proven invaluable. We are extremely stable. When things get confusing or awkward or there's been a misunderstanding, he turns to her for advice and guidance. Everybody works together to keep us all positive. The Goddess Indigo helps bridge those events that just need another person's viewpoint and perspective. I realize that his first duty is to her, and I do everything I can to make him look good, and I'd do whatever I could for her. So, there's never been any stress with him having a

Master. It's just part of the deal, and she actively supports our relationship.

Dr. Bob Rubel: There are many good books on authority-imbalanced dynamics, power exchange relationships, and other topics useful for those in sophisticated relationship structures. I'd venture to say — the more familiar you are with the literature of this subculture, the more stable your relationship is likely to be.

constants: Oh, that brings up another point. Another way his autism manifests involves his fixation on reading, research, and writing. He gets extremely focused on whatever interests him in the moment. For example, when he starts reading a new book, he is as enthusiastic and focused on that as one can be. He highlights sentences and paragraphs, reread it, take notes, write in the margins, tells me about it, reads passages from it. You get the idea. He gets very *driven* when he takes on a new project. He requires a lot of uninterrupted time to himself. In fact, he is extremely reclusive and prefers being isolated. We seldom go out. This is a little hard on me, as I'm an extrovert. He encourages me to go to lunches or diners with my own friends or family. He does not come along.

At six o'clock, things stop and we begin preparing for our evening together. We shower, change clothes and such. Once this ritual has begun, he becomes very, very focused on me. I'm his slave every evening. Now, there's a "carve-out" for his time with The Goddess Indigo. If she calls, I stop everything until they're off the phone. Sometimes she gives him a task to do; other times she is asking his opinion about something. We try to have dinner with her every Tuesday night. There are also "carve-out" times so I can be with other people. I must take care of that part of me. If I don't, I'll start sinking. He recognizes that.

But there is nothing so wonderful as being the special interest of someone on the Spectrum! He's very intense and has created the magical environment in which we live. Being the center of his imaginary universe is pretty darn awesome.

Dr. Bob Rubel: And our first toast at dinner *every* night is: "Happy Valentine's Day, babygirl."

Our second toast (that she initiates) is: "To our protocols, that keep us ever-mindful of the *magic* of our relationship."

The third toast is quite special, and I've been using it nightly since I first developed it in 2012: "To our Leather brethren, everywhere." I say this to recognize the Leather community that has illuminated the Path enabling me to be what I am today.

The Dual ASD Power Exchange
Relationship

Interview with Mama Silky and Kitten

Kitten: I'm Silky's Kitten, and Mama Silky and I have been together for five years. I have some interesting perspectives on this, because in my vanilla life I'm a psychologist. I am Silky's collared slave, but we're not really high protocol or completely 24/7.

Mama Silky: I think of high protocol as a micromanaging thing, and I'm not really good at that. I'm not as good as they are with handling people. I'm a retired IT professional, so I kind of fit the stereotype of someone on the autism spectrum. I got a degree in computers because I don't understand people.

Kitten: And I got a PhD in psychology because I'm on the autism spectrum and I wanted to be able to understand people! I just don't have a neurotypical understanding of them. Between the two of us, I'm the one who brings in the income. I think a lot of people assume that the dominant would be the one to make the money; they have that 1950's household idea. But I earn the income and she takes care of the house.

Mama Silky: Basically, I work my butt off too, but I don't get paid for it. I do the shopping and take the car to the mechanic and deal with the landlord when something needs to be repaired. They pay all the bills. This is the way we like to divide it up, even though it's not stereotypical. I do like to tell people what to do, but I don't like all that high-protocol stuff.

Kitten: Our power exchange does come in the most when we play together. I'm not saying it's only sexual though; it's much more than that. Sometimes part of my service to her is being the executive function for the two of us.

Mama Silky: We tend to divide up the executive functioning depending on who is good at what part of it. I may be the dominant and they may be the submissive, but this is also very much a partnership.

Kitten: I'm forty-eight, non-binary, my pronouns are they/them, and I'm still trying to find more specific language to describe the aspects of that. When we first got together, I thought I was more of an ally of the trans community. I actually did my dissertation back in 2006 about therapy with transgender people. I just thought that I had an affinity with them, and I didn't realize that I was drawn to that work for reasons related to my own identity. Sometimes I feel like I have some agender mixed in there. But I'm fascinated with other people's gender, and I'm still trying to figure out what gives me gender euphoria. I'm not medically transitioned, although I am very subtly socially transitioned; I express more androgyny than I used to. I recently got a septum piercing, and that gave me a lot of gender euphoria for some reason, but I still find myself hard to define. We actually got together because I was starting to explore that aspect of myself more. But I'm very drawn to femme dominant types.

Mama Silky: And I do qualify as the gentle femme-dom. I'm sixty, and I was assigned male at birth, but I have some intersex traits. I was born in the early 1960s and we think I might be one of the DES babies. I am very much transgender, possibly intersex, and my pronouns are She/Her. I'm still trying to figure out my sexuality, though, because I suspect I have some asexual tendencies. I know that my concept of sex is not the same as everybody else's, but I don't know exactly what that means. We found each other in middle age—we were married to other people when we met and we're married to each other now—so you can imagine that was an interesting year. The old Chinese curse—may you live in interesting times!

I make the decisions about what we do when we're at home together, but the other major parts of their life are their work and their medical issues, and I don't like to interfere with those unless they ask me to, because I don't feel right making choices about someone else's body. Generally, though, they're pretty good at saying, "I need to do such-and-such," and I'll say, "OK, then go do it." For example, they had a situation with kidney stones last week, and we dropped everything and took them to the ER twice, because we wanted to make sure they were OK. But I don't think of that as having authority over it, I just think of it as me making sure it gets done. My big goal is for them to be happy, and as long as they're happy, I'm OK.

Kitten: In some of the areas of our life, we have a more collaborative egalitarian relationship; it's the more intimate parts of my life where she has more power and authority. She's done a lot of controlling my appearance in the past, but lately that's fallen away due to medical problems. I had foot and ankle surgery a few months ago, and I had to stop shaving my legs and underarms. I'd been keeping all that smooth for her, because she prefers a lack of body hair. But then during my surgery recovery, and since, I had to stop. And that's surprisingly given me a little bit of gender euphoria, so I don't know if I want to go back. So we negotiate on things like that.

In terms of our autism, both of us were diagnosed more recently, late in life. (You won't hear me using the term ASD, because I don't consider it a disorder, I consider it just another neurotype, which is part of human diversity.) I love to hear these twenty-year-olds saying that they were late-diagnosed! Supposedly anyone diagnosed as an adult is "late", but I lived almost five decades of my life not knowing this about myself. And ten-plus years of being a licensed psychologist was not helpful in figuring out that I'm autistic!

I'm high-masking, and I've always worked with adults rather than children. When I finished my dissertation in 2006, people were thinking of autism as only the low-functioning end; that if you weren't identified in childhood, it wasn't bad enough to be actual autism. The idea of adults being diagnosed is relatively new as far as I can tell. I even worked at a camp for autistic kids the summer before I started college. I did have an affinity for working with them, but I also found it very difficult, because we were doing what I now know to be applied behavioral analysis. I had a hard time implementing it, and looking back I realize that I had a strong emotional reaction to inflicting it on these kids.

But for most of my life, all I knew was that I was really good at academic pursuits—most teachers liked having me in class—but while I had some friends, a lot of people thought I was weird. I would get excited and talk too much and too loudly. But in the early '90s, people thought that autism looked like *Rain Man*, or someone who was nonverbal and stimming in an obvious way. I just knew that I annoyed people, without meaning to.

A few years ago, I started doing trauma therapy for myself. Here another one for you: I didn't know I had complex PTSD until a few years ago. The way the human mind can compartmentalize can be shocking! The people I'd grown up around told me that I overexaggerated everything and I was too sensitive, and I believed all that up until a few years ago. I was reading a lot about C-PTSD, which is not even in the DSM at this time, and as I was finding information and online communities, I found people who were talking about neurodiversity. That was new to me at the time, and I started reading more about it, and I found a lot of people who were late-diagnosed autistic adults. Reading their words was the first time I had ever heard about autism described from the inside, and it resonated with the "private me" which I tried to hide from most people.

In my opinion, the DSM and its predecessors describe autism from the outside, and a lot of those behaviors are what autistic people do when they are distressed. Growing up, I was shamed so badly for acting distressed that I learned to mask it. Even in grad school, in my clinical training, I was told, "Be yourself ... but don't do any of these things, and for God's sake don't forget to do these things," which meant I couldn't be myself. It was a subtle neurotypical bias, with people expecting me to know how to act in ways that I didn't understand. I just thought that I had to try harder, because everyone else seems to be getting this, and they tell me this is what a psychologist is supposed to be. Because of this, it took me a lot longer to get my doctorate, but I was very determined. Looking back, I probably burned myself out, but I wanted this career and I got there.

I've developed a reputation in my workplace for doing well with people who are "difficult clients", and I love doing that. Many of them are probably neurodivergent in some way, whether that's autism or

ADHD or something like that. If you think about it, neurodivergent just means that your mind doesn't work in a way that the world is designed for. So in some ways being autistic worked well for my field, because I can really dive headfirst into the areas that interest me—like gender diversity or psychoeducation—and it's using autistic info-dumping as a positive thing; it becomes a special interest.

Anyway, a psychologist in my community was doing a class on diagnosing autism in adults, and I called and asked her to assess me. Fortunately she took my insurance! I didn't need a full assessment because I wasn't expecting to need accommodations or to go on disability. So we did a two-session extended clinical interview, and at the end of it she said, "Yeah, you're autistic." And at the same time I was looking into this, I was also telling Mama Silky, "Hey some of this fits me, but it fits you too!"

Mama Silky: I'd been wondering about it for a long time, actually. You get used to "This is just how my life is. Doesn't everybody feel this way?" I've been in one LARP for something like thirty years, and I've met so many people who are on the spectrum that I started wondering about myself. But it took me a long time to find someone who could test me. They said I was definitely on the spectrum, and actually that I was far enough over that I probably needed a lot of help.

With our relationship, the worst thing about my autism is that I'm not always the best at communicating, and I'll say the wrong thing. I actually had a situation where we were watching an episode of *Chopped*, and I tried to make a comment about using sweet potato, and I said "candy corn" instead of "sweet potato". So those kinds of mistakes can be pretty confusing. Add to that the fact that I understand computers and machines better than I understand people, and it's a lot of effort to keep up the right amount of communication.

Kitten: The thing to understand about our dynamic is that even though we're both autistic, we have two different presentations of it. Mama Silky struggles more with the executive function parts of it, and I struggle more with emotional dysregulation. If you were to meet me at work, you would never guess that because I'm good at masking, but behind closed doors it's a different story. I'm sensory-seeking in the sense that I'm a fairly heavy masochist. I love all those intense sensations; they quiet down my nervous system. I'm more adventurous with food; she likes to eat the same things all the time. She's sensory-avoidant in that way.

Mama Silky: But I do love hurting her. If I don't get BDSM on a semi-regular basis, I start feeling weird. Sadism calms me like masochism calms her. I get something from absorbing their pain. It's an energy exchange. I'm something of a psychic vampire, and I feed off of the pain. One of their tattoos is my symbol on her butt cheek, and I love looking at that, knowing I've done the equivalent of tattooing my name on them.

Kitten: Both of us came to realize that BDSM is part of our toolkit for our emotional regulation and our sensory diet. When I had foot surgery and we couldn't play for a couple of weeks, that was rough. But part of her authority over me is that she tells me No. I want all the masochistic things, even when it's not good for me at the moment. I'll say "I want to try this!" and she'll say, "No, we need to learn more about that," or "No, that's not safe."

Mama Silky: The last time we went to a kink convention, I just chased them around making sure that they didn't do anything unsafe. I made sure I was there when they played with other people.

It's not like we don't have any problems—sometimes things just don't go well, and I think that does have to do with us being on the spectrum.

Kitten: We also both have trauma histories, although it's hard to find a neurodivergent person who doesn't have a trauma history, because the neurotypical-centric world can be extremely invalidating. Both of us had experiences growing up where our autism was not welcome. But the dynamic does give us a sense of structure. Even my gender identity exploration is negotiated through the dynamic—for a long time she called me her little girl, and now I'm her little one.

Mama Silky: I may be the dominant here, but I'm only the dominant as long as they want that. They have to be happy with it too.

Kitten: My advice to people who are looking for a power exchange partner, and who are looking at someone on the spectrum who understands their own neurotype, would be to keep an open mind and go slowly when exploring limits. Their boundaries might not be what you expect them to be! For example, if they go nonverbal during play, that might be strange for you. People with an autistic neurotype may have extremes with talking—all or nothing. When I'm in a rational frame of mind, I'm very verbal and I use lots of words, but it's typical for me to go nonverbal during play. We have to arrange some hand signals for that.

When you grow up autistic, you often get told that you're weird, or unacceptable, or you don't try hard enough, or you're overly sensitive, or too picky about food. You may have to build things up very slowly while keeping an eye on their emotional state. What happens when their cognition shifts? You might have to careful of that with a neurotypical person as well, but autistic people may have unusual experiences when it comes to altered states of consciousness. Understand that their sensory experiences may be unusual as well. Something that other people perceive as really extreme could have an autistic person saying, "Oh, wow, that's really cool!"

Mama Silky: And vice versa! Something you might think would be no big deal will actually be a really big deal for them. You have to be careful, and you have to go slow, because you don't know where their trigger points are going to be.

Kitten: And you don't know where the trauma points are going to be! Trauma is not stored in the brain in words. It's saved in sensory impressions and physical sensations, and you might stumble across that in kink sooner than in other places. I recommend that the two of you put together a "what if everything goes to shit" plan. Go ahead and say, "if an abreaction happens, here's what we're going to do." And even with that, you still might have some trial and error. We discovered that when I'm in my rational mind, I can say, "I like this and I don't like that." But if I'm in an altered state, which happens to me when we're playing, it's a totally different story. Subspace me is not the same as ordinary-conversation me.

Their needs for aftercare might also be different. Everyone thinks that cuddling is the absolute go-to, but if you're someone who spends a lot of time in sensory overwhelm, you might need some alone time afterwards. It's good if they already know their sensory profile and can communicate that. Another part which can be tricky is that many of us have trouble putting feelings into words. That's a skill which can be learned, so focus on debriefing afterwards. The autistic person might not be able to say that they were sad or overwhelmed or whatever, but they might be able to recount the sensations they felt in their body. Also, the way they talk about their bodily experience might be very different.

And then there's the meltdowns! Not all autistic people have meltdowns, but a lot of us do. That's a difference between us—I have meltdowns and she really doesn't.

Mama Silky: At the moment, my medication works! But the problem is that when they have a meltdown, they become a lot louder than I'm used to, and that hits my sensory stuff.

Kitten: I want to emphasize that an autistic meltdown is different from what most people think of when they say "meltdown". Neurotypical people think of it like an emotional temper tantrum, where for us it means that something has gone very wrong with our neurology and it's more involuntary. The fight/flight/freeze part of the brain is lit up like a Christmas tree, and the rational mind is just not there. I think I may be more prone to them because I'm the one who has a paid job working with people all the time, coping with hierarchy and all those unwritten rules and expectations, and that can build up. Some of us don't have meltdowns, we have shutdowns, which is like an internal meltdown where the person withdraws from everything. So when someone's having a meltdown or a shutdown, that's not the time to debrief or renegotiate the dynamic. That's a time to try to find safety and quiet.

Mama Silky: When that happens, you can't order them to stop. Sometimes you can't order them to do anything. That never works. I have to work with them and help them ride it through. When they get out the other end of it, I help them recover. I've never seen them feel good about it afterwards, either. Most of the time they're embarrassed by what happened, and it's my job to say, "No, it's OK, you don't have to feel bad, I understand this just happens."

Kitten: So have some contingency plans for incidents like that. Also, remember that when we're into something, we're *really* into it. If an autistic person in into pet play, there will be times when *everything* is about pet play. I think that's why there are so many of us in these communities. BDSM and power exchange are activities we can just dive headfirst into. We can present and volunteer at conferences, we can give talks, we can mentor other people, we can read all the books about it. These things lend themselves well to becoming special interests. We're erotic geeks. I know a lot of people in the kink scene who are asexual, but they're all about unusual ways of being erotic and sensual. In the BDSM world, you can define "sex" and "erotic" and "intimate" and "sensual" in so many different ways! There are so many variations that someone asexual can still be involved.

Mama Silky: I remember the first time we played at one of the local dungeons. They reached up and kissed me while we were playing, and it was electrifying, an amazing connection. And we never looked back after that.

Interview with Daddy Krys and Jamie

Jamie: Believe it or not, we met on Fetlife. I was brand new to the community and scrolling through profiles which were local to me. I came across their profile and everything about it sounded like everything I wanted when I first started exploring kink. I particularly remember a phrase in the profile— "gentle domination"—which really piqued my interest, so we got to chatting. What started as a play session turned into what's now a three-year relationship. Our power exchange has slowly evolved into a TPE relationship over time.

Krys: All decisions ultimately come to me, and I choose with my best intentions for her. The choice to do that was a completely mutual one. It happened slowly where more and more power was handed over.

Jamie: I know that Daddy had some trepidation around doing that at first, because of not-so-great experiences in past relationships. My only caveat was that I need to be able to say what my thoughts and opinions are about any decision, but I will abide by their decision, because I know that at the end of the day Daddy has my best interests at heart and is looking out for me. That was reassuring to them, as was taking things slowly.

Krys: When I first met her, I was not looking for another power dynamic. In fact, I'd just finished a power dynamic which was not healthy at all, so I was very hesitant. But she's just such a good girl that I couldn't forgive myself if I passed over her service.

I was diagnosed with autism when I was eleven years old. I was a very oppositional child, a "troublemaker" all the time. I went through a variety of early diagnoses before a doctor who was able to see the whole picture finally said, "This is clearly autism". Therapy and my journey in learning coping mechanisms for my brain ultimately turned into a special interest in human psychology and observation of other humans. I just love people-watching; We are such interesting creatures.

Jamie: I haven't been officially diagnosed with autism, but we are pretty certain that I have it. There are lots of indicators of my "neuro-spicies". (I have been diagnosed with major depressive disorder.) I don't feel that it needs to be diagnosed; It is just part of who I am. I love the TPE aspect of our relationship because I've always done better when I have clear direction—when I know what I'm supposed to do, and I just get told to do it. I like having free thought—I have free thoughts!—but I do best when I am guided and led on a path. I'm very prone to getting distracted and hyper fixated on things which really aren't that important and often, I won't have the perspective to figure that out by myself. Having someone to keep me on track is very important.

Krys: Structure is very important to her; If she doesn't have structure, she'll start to crumble a little bit.

Jamie: A lot, actually.

Krys: The structured nature of these relationships is one hundred per cent what drew me to them. Having clear expectations about what we are doing in the relationship. The ability to communicate what's on my mind, to have it acknowledged and received and having that not be awkward. For a lot of allistic folks, directness is a forbidden thing—you must dance around whatever point you're trying to make. I would prefer just to put it out there and move forward from that. This relationship structure has really helped, because it normalizes me having that directness, that voice.

Here I get to be myself and not mask. Other relationships I've been in, I feel like I still must mask a little bit. Finding someone else who is also autistic works so well. We run in groups; I think. We clump together and find each other.

Jamie: I have a strong desire to communicate; I have a hard time sitting on thoughts and feelings. They're coming out of my mouth one way or another, so I'd rather just talk about them when they come up. Sitting on them makes everyone uncomfortable because it's very clear when I'm trying not to say something. That's a learned skill I've had to develop because people don't generally like to hear things in the moment, but I always feel like I have to say whatever it is right away. But being like this helps one hundred per cent with transparency! I don't feel like I must hide anything—I don't *want* to hide anything.

Krys: I'm one of those autistic humans who is always very empathetic—actually more like a giant gaping empathetic wound. I can see the path people are walking and I can feel it. I find that it helps a lot with a Dominant perspective. I can quickly get a feel for someone and figure out what is required for their mental health. So that's another advantage of my autism.

Jamie: On the other hand, there are the mental fixations. I see something shiny, and I'm going to fixate on it and study nothing else for three weeks. I'll learn everything I can about it, and not pay attention to other things which may be more important. That can be a detriment.

Krys: But it does give you so many interesting skills, and you have so much knowledge in your brain.

Jamie: From a practical point of view, it can be useful but it's not as good for stability in a relationship. I can become obsessed with things, "Oh, this job looks interesting! I'm going to completely uproot my career to try out this new job!" Our relationship style helps compensate for that—Daddy won't let me do stupid things—but it is part of the "neurospicy" problems.

Krys: Her most recent special interest was going to the northern point of British Columbia to a very isolated little island resort and working there for six months out of the year. I'm in favor of some of that, but we must slow it down just a little bit. Sensory issues can also be difficult, especially if one person is very sensory-seeking and the other is more sensory-withdrawn. That must be acknowledged and communicated very well.

Jamie: When mental health is in a slump it can become harder to maintain where I want to be—and where they want me to be. Sometimes we must renegotiate some of the minor points of our dynamic on the fly, on a day-to-day basis; although not the overarching things.

Krys: Nothing is absolutely set in stone, because if she's having a really bad day, I need to be able to ask what's going on and adjust things. That's something we've learned to do.

For people who are just getting into this, I want to mention the rigid black-and-white thinking that can be barrier. In all my life, I've never met anyone who is more dedicated to me than Jamie is. The dedication and consistency are wonderful. But there's that black-and white "This is good behavior, and this is bad behavior. I want to be good," which can get us into those ruts of thinking, so you need to work on that and break those thoughts down and apart. Allistic folks tend to be more malleable and nuanced in their thoughts and not so black and white.

Jamie: Look for those gray areas! Don't get caught up in "This is explicitly good" and "This is explicitly bad." That was something I struggled with at the start. This is good and this is bad, but what about everything in between? Where does that fall? I had to learn that it doesn't have to be categorized; it can just be what it is. (But I've also just been slowly moving many of them over to the bad or good side.) I have a list!

Krys: Oh, she does love lists!

Jamie: It's also important to write things together. Write as much down as you can; this not only helps with the black-and-white thinking, but also the ability to go back and reexamine it. I like having something tangible to remember and remind me of the expectations.

Krys: For the times when they can't communicate—moments of "shutdown"—they can keep a journal. Writing back and forth that way is a great idea. Picking up some ASL for those moments can also work well. It's especially good in the dungeon, during play when someone might go nonverbal. It works quite well.

Jamie: I feel like a hypocrite for saying this, because it's not exactly what we did, but taking things as slow as possible is important for people on the spectrum. We started seeing each other right at the beginning of the pandemic, so we ended up isolating and going into lockdown together. So, it's a little hypocritical for me to say that new folks should take things slowly, but honestly you can end up hyper fixating on people as well as hobbies. You need to balance the new relationship energy with respecting everyone's boundaries and consent. Start with a single negotiation, maybe a single play session.

Krys: I think that the media often tends to portray autistic folks as emotionless. I know that my face doesn't give off much in the way of emotional signals, but I believe that we can be very emotional, and very empathetic. I think it's a prize and a privilege to have someone open to you as completely as an autistic person can. People on the spectrum are beautiful humans, and we have many gifts that haven't yet been acknowledged.

Appendices

Appendix I: Recommended Reading on ASD

Recommended by ASD people we know!

- ❖ Devon Price: *Unmasking Autism*
- ❖ Nick Walker: *Neuroqueer Heresies*
- ❖ Jenara Nerenburg: *Divergent Mind*
- ❖ Joanne Limburg: *Letters to My Weird Sisters*
- ❖ Eric Garcia: *We're Not Broken*

- ❖ https://wrongplanet.net/
- ❖ https://aucademy.co.uk/
- ❖ https://embrace-autism.com/
- ❖ https://autisticadvocacy.org/
- ❖ https://autisticgirlsnetwork.org/
- ❖ https://soyoureautistic.com/masking-camouflaging-mimicking/
- ❖ https://neuroclastic.com/

Appendix II: Dr. Bob Rubel's Book List

Here is a list of the four books I most recommend if you have or live with someone who has Asperger Syndrome:

❖ Maxine Aston and Rudy Simone. *22 Things a Woman Must Know If She Loves a Man With Asperger's Syndrome.*

❖ David Finch. *The Journal of Best Practices: A Memoir of Marriage, Asperger Syndrome, and One Man's Quest to Be a Better Husband.*

❖ Temple Grandin and Sean Barron. *The Unwritten Rules of Social Relationships: Decoding Social Mysteries Through the Unique Perspectives of Autism.*

❖ Katrin Bentley *Alone Together: Making an Asperger Marriage Work.*

These are books that have profoundly influenced the way I think over the past five years or so.

❖ Kathryn Schultz. *Being Wrong: Adventures in the Margin of Error.*

❖ Gary van Warmerdam. *MindWorks.* And his online course: PathwayToHappiness.com, which I *highly* recommend. It is a course in self-mastery.

❖ Malcolm Gladwell. *The Tipping Point, Blink, Outliers.*

❖ Seth Godin. *The Dip.* (Very small but amazing book about knowing when to quit in order not to squander your time and attention. It contains models that apply to relationships. Good book to have around.)

❖ Robert Maurer. *The Spirit of Kaizen: Creating Lasting Excellence One Small Step at a Time.* (This is *the* book about creating incremental change. This is "necessary reading" for leaders.)

❖ Daniel Kahneman. *Thinking, Fast and Slow.* (I'm now on my third pass through this book on Audible Books and highlighting the book, itself. One of the most profound books I've ever read. Lots of insight about things you think you know, about which you are sooooo wrong.)

❖ The Arbinger Institute. *Leadership and Self-Deception.* (Very important book.)

❖ The Great Courses series. *Your Deceptive Mind.* (Outstanding wake-up call for those of us who think we actually are making choices and actually "know" things.)

❖ Stephen Covey. *Seven Habits of Highly Effective People.* (There is an accompanying workbook sold separately.)

❖ R.G.H. Siu. *The Craft of Power.*

❖ Spencer Johnson. *Who Moved my Cheese?* (On flexibility.)

❖ Thomas M. Sterner. *The Practicing Mind.* (On mindfulness.)

❖ Jan Chozen Bays, MD. *How to Train a Wild Elephant (and other lessons in mindfulness).* (This book includes 52 practice exercises.)

❖ Terry Fadem. *The Art of Asking: Ask Better Questions, Get Better Answers.* (Teaches how to overcome one's tendency to become reactive by asking questions that reveal the other person's intent.)

❖ Marlene LeFever. *Learning Styles.* (Basic read for anyone trying to teach/train someone else.)

❖ John Navarro. *What Every Body is Saying.* (25-year FBI interrogator—this is about body language.)

❖ Pace and Kyeli. *The Usual Error: Why We Don't Understand Each Other and 14 Ways to Make It Better.*

❖ Kerry Patterson, Joseph Grenny, *et als. Crucial Conversations: Tools for Talking When the Stakes are High.*

❖ Rick Foster and Greg Hicks. *How We Choose to be Happy.*

❖ Richard Bandler and John LaValle. *Persuasion Engineering.* (Bandler was the co-creator of the concept of Neuro-Linguistic Programming with *Frogs to Princes.*)

❖ Sean Young. *Stick With It: A Scientifically Proven Process for Changing Your Life—For Good.*

❖ Theron Q. Dumont. *The Master Mind: The Key to Mental Power, Development, and Efficiency.*

❖ Brian Tracy. *How the Best Leaders Lead.*

❖ Brené Brown. *The Gifts of Imperfection: Let Go of Who You Think You're Supposed to Be and Embrace Who You Are.*

- ❖ Barry Schwartz. *The Paradox of Choice: Why More Is Less.* (I adopted this viewpoint in certain aspects of my own M/s dynamic.)
- ❖ Martin Yate. *Knock 'em Dead Job Interview.* (First 50 pages or so are dead-on descriptions of what you need to do to establish and maintain a relationship. Particularly relevant to M/s relationships.)
- ❖ Eric Berne, MD. *What Do You Say After You Say Hello? The Psychology of Human Destiny.* (You mainly need the first 27 pages of Part I. Very useful perspective on relationships.)
- ❖ Phil M. Jones. *Exactly What to Say: The Magic Words for Influence and Impact.* (You'd be amazed how you can influence others by using phrases you've known all your life but never considered to be "tools".)
- ❖ Sonja Lyubomirsky. *The How of Happiness: A New Approach to Getting the Life You Want.* (She is a psych professor. This book deconstructs the elements of "happiness".)
- ❖ Rintu Basu. *Persuasion Skills Black Book: Practical NLP Language Patterns for Getting the Response You Want.* (What an amazing book. It manages to boil down the absolutely essential NLP "sleight-of-mouth" language patterns into a small book. Total "meat" from page to page. Would take you many years to derive these lessons.)
- ❖ Olivia Fox Cabane. *The Charisma Myth: How Anyone Can Master the Art and Science of Personal Magnetism.* (Author is a senior lecturer in this field. This material was originally developed for Harvard and Yale courses. Breaks down the process into bite-sized pieces.)
- ❖ Mark Leary. *Understanding the Mysteries of Human Behavior Course Guidebook.* (This is an audio book, part of the Great Courses series. The book is at the 501-level. It answers very interesting questions, such as: "Where do people's personalities come from?" I highly recommend this book.)
- ❖ David J. Lieberman. *Never be Lied to Again: How to get the Truth in 5 Minutes or Less in Any Conversation or Situation.*

Appendix III: Dr. Bob and The Goddess Indigo's Recommended List of Tests and Quizzes

Compiled by The Goddess Indigo and Dr. Bob: GoddessAndDoc@Gmail.com

The following exercises offer interesting and useful personal insights. Many of the results are immediately applicable to you and those close to you. If you have other tests and quizzes you think we should know about and include on this list, please send them to Dr. Bob at PowerExchangeEditor@Yahoo.com.

Identifying your core values:

https://kaleidoscopeaxiom.com/krystallos-app

This process can take a while. I think it took me a number of hours. It's not that it's hard, it's that it's tedious. They keep asking you to make choices and associations between words. At the end, though, you will gain great insight into what you value and how these "concept words" are connected in your brain. What I found so interesting is that the way *my* words were connected was quite different than the way my Master's or my babygirl's words were connected. Which is the point, after all.

https://www.cmu.edu/career/documents/careerguides/myCareerPathGuide2 018-2019.pdf See "Values Exercise."

https://sparketype.com/

Tests/quizzes you can take to gain more personal insight.

Personality (Myers/Briggs)

https://16Personalities.com

This is my personal favorite, as once you know your four-letter MBTI (Myers/Briggs Type Indicator) and plug yours and your partner's scores into an Internet search, it will tell you quite a bit about your combined strengths and weaknesses. When Master and I did this, the results sounded rather like a "final report" of a psychotherapist who had been working with us for years. Really eerie.

Personal strengths

https://www.gallup.com/cliftonstrengths/en/252137/home.aspx
Clifton Strengths Assessment by the Gallup organization. Note: I *highly* recommend that everyone involved in your dynamic take this test. I have also hired their coach to review implications for interacting with my Master and my slave. Very interesting insights in this one.

Learning modality

https://www.thoughtco.com/learning-style-quiz-4076781
https://www.vark-learn.com
https://www. howtolearn.com
https://www.howtolearn.com/learning-styles-quiz/

Apology Quiz

https://5lovelanguages.com/quizzes/apology-language

Anger Quiz

https://5lovelanguages.com/quizzes/anger-assessment

Problem solving and work-style professional test:

https://www.kolbe.com/kolbe-a-index/
Note: there is a $55 cost. This test reveals individual strengths in a work setting. In structured relationships, it will give the Leader valuable information about four major components about strong/weak areas in relation to project completion tasks.

Strength-finding test:

https://www.redbull.com/int-en/wingfinder
This is remarkably comprehensive and free. It takes about 35 minutes.

DISCE Personality Profile

https://discpersonalitytesting.com/free-disc-test/

Stress Level Test

https://psychcentral.com/quizzes/stress-test

"Why Do I Love Them So Much" Quiz

https://www.marriage.com/quizzes/why-do-i-love-them-so-much-quiz

What's Your Conflict Style in a Relationship?

https://www.marriage.com/quizzes/whats-your-conflict-style-in-a-relationship-quiz

Who Loves Who More?

https://www.marriage.com/quizzes/who-loves-more-quiz

What Kind of Couple Are You Quiz

https://www.marriage.com/quizzes/what-kind-of-couple-are-you-quiz

Long Distance Relationships

https://getlasting.com/long-distance-relationships
https://www.modernlovelongdistance.com/long-distance-relationship-activities/

Source for more tests/quizzes:

https://www.authentichappiness.sas.upenn.edu/testcenter

There are many quick tests to take on here. Categories include: Emotion questionnaires, Engagement questionnaires. Flourishing questionnaires, Life satisfaction questionnaires, Meaning questionnaires.